In terms of an introducti___ _____ ___ ___ ___ ___ and exercise of the pap_ ___ ___ ___ ___ ___ ___ this book and you will ga___ ___ ___ ___ ___ ___ ___ many Christians is a mystery, now unpacked by a trusted evangelical theologian and pastor.

Gregg R. Allison
Professor of Christian Theology,
The Southern Baptist Theological Seminary, Louisville, Kentucky

With Pope Francis prominently in the news, we are forced to confront the whole idea of the papacy. Many Christians either reject everything about it out of hand, or they romantically embrace individual heroes such as John Paul II. Professor De Chirico investigate the phenomenon of Roman Catholic hierarchy using biblical exegesis, fascinating historical data, and basic theological insights to inform our view. He alerts us to the great dangers involved in the hierarchical model, while at the same time pleading for a proper kind of church unity. Engaging, clearly written, polemical in the best sense, and resolutely Scriptural, this is easily the best shorter guide for those wanting to know how to evaluate the institution of the papacy and related matters.

William Edgar
Professor of Apologetics,
Westminster Theological Seminary, Philadelphia, Pennsylvania

How readable! How fascinating! How important! This book is a page-turner. I kept thinking, 'I have it, to whom can I give it?' People came to mind. We live in days when the current pope is a popular man, even Time magazine's 'Man of the Year' in 2013. What does it do for his spiritual condition day by day to consider himself to be the number one vicarious representative in the cosmos of the Son of God? This book asks, "Is this true?" Then it concludes from examining the history of the papacy that it is not so. Right at the heart of Roman Catholicism there is this giant delusion. You don't believe me? Then read this fascinating and brief book and think for yourself.

Geoff Thomas
Aberystwyth Baptist Church, Aberystwyth, Wales

A CHRISTIAN'S POCKET GUIDE TO

THE PAPACY

ITS ORIGIN AND ROLE IN THE 21ST CENTURY

LEONARDO DE CHIRICO

CHRISTIAN
FOCUS

Copyright © Leonardo De Chirico 2015

paperback ISBN 978-1-78191-299-7
epub ISBN 978-1-78191-609-4
Mobi ISBN 978-1-78191-610-0

Published in 2015
by
Christian Focus Publications Ltd,
Geanies House, Fearn, Ross-shire,
IV20 1TW, Scotland, Great Britain
www.christianfocus.com

Cover design by Daniel van Straaten

Printed by Norhaven, Denmark

CONTENTS

⚠ Warning
𝄋 Don't Forget
⑦ Stop and Think
☀ Point of Interest

PREFACE

TIME magazine named Pope Francis 'Person of the Year' 2013. The main reason for his nomination was his 'rejection of luxury.' The Pope's unassuming personality and style makes him one of the most popular figures in the contemporary celebrity culture. Francis is seen as a Pope for whom dogma is less important than attitude, mercy more relevant than truth, and generosity of spirit more apt than affirming traditional belief. Yet he stands on the living tradition of one of the world's most ancient institutions, which has generated binding 'dogmas' and a very traditional set of moral codes, thus shaping Western civilization and heading the largest religious group in the world—the Roman Catholic Church.

There are several ways of looking at the papacy beyond common places and media caricatures. This book will try to answer the following introductory questions: Who are the Popes and how does the Roman Catholic Church define their role? How could a leadership position in the Christian church come to have such an 'imperial' shape? Why was Rome so important in that process? What was the role of history in the development of the Papacy? How did the Protestant Reformers of the sixteenth century and beyond view it? What about the present-day Popes? What is the ecumenical significance of the Papacy and what are its prospects in the global world? These and other questions will form the background to our inquiry into the Biblical, historical, and theological fabric of the Papacy.

I wish to express my gratitude to my friend Reid Karr who was extremely helpful in reading the manuscript and in suggesting improvements. The remaining oddities are my responsibility.

This work is part of my ongoing attempt to grasp what is the theological core of the Roman Catholic vision. I lecture in historical theology at IFED (Istituto di Formazione Evangelica e Documentazione, Padua, Italy) where I regularly teach courses on patristic, Roman Catholic and contemporary theology. My PhD thesis was on Evangelical interpretations of Vatican II, the most important twentieth-century event in the Roman Catholic Church.[1] Studying Popes' encyclicals and documents was, and still is, part of my professional job, which I thoroughly enjoy. I write occasional reports on Roman Catholicism (the 'Vatican files'), where I survey events and trends emerging from the Vatican.[2] In my works on Roman Catholicism I try to analyze whatever I write about as part of a theological 'whole'. I will try to do the same in this study on the Papacy.

This book is dedicated to the brothers and sisters of the Evangelical Church Breccia di Roma, where I have served as pastor since 2010. Their fellowship and friendship in the gospel is a source of ongoing strength for me. The mission of our church is to be a 'priestly, kingly, and prophetic community' in Rome by being a Reformed witness in a city where the Papacy is considered the highest expression of 'hard' power and where the Roman Church is the main religious, social, and economic player. We feel like grasshoppers in a land of giants (Num. 13:33), but it is thrilling to see the gospel working out its 'soft' power in people's lives and in society. We try to accomplish our mission having the Word of God as our supreme standard (*sola Scriptura*). Across the centuries, Popes have also wanted to exercise the roles of priests, kings and prophets in their own absolute way. May this book serve as an encouragement to be critical and self-critical in the way we seek to fulfil our priestly, kingly, and prophetic callings.

1

WE HAVE A POPE!

HABEMUS PAPAM!

THE PAPAL OFFICE
THROUGH HIS TITLES AND SYMBOLS

'*Gaudium Magnum: Habemus Papam!*' These famous words introduce a new Pope to the world. They are spoken to the throng that gathers in St. Peter's Square to celebrate the occasion. The Pope is one of the last examples of absolute sovereignty in the modern world and embodies one of history's oldest institutions. The executive, legislative, and juridical powers are all concentrated in the Papal office. Until the Pope dies or resigns, he remains the Pope with all his titles and privileges. The only restriction on his power is that he cannot choose his own successor. In other words, the papacy is not dynastic. This task belongs to the College of electing Cardinals, that is, cardinals under eighty years old. They gather to elect a new Pope in the 'Conclave' (from the Latin *cum clave*, i.e. locked up with a key), located in the Sistine Chapel. If the Pope cannot choose his own successor he can, nonetheless, choose those who elect.

A good starting point for investigating the significance of the Papacy is the 1994 *Catechism of the Catholic Church*. It is the most recent and comprehensive account of the Roman Catholic faith. Referring to the office of the Pope, the *Catechism* notes in paragraph 882 that 'the Roman Pontiff, by reason of his office as Vicar of Christ, and as pastor of the entire Church has full, supreme, and universal power over the whole Church, a power which he can always exercise unhindered.'[3] This brief sentence contains an apt summary of what the history and office of the papacy are all about. The Pope is a contemporary religious leader who boasts of direct and unbroken lineage to the Apostle Peter. The Pope, by means of succession, claims to continue the mission entrusted to Peter.

Further reinforcing his power and authority, paragraph 937 of the *Catechism* states: 'The Pope enjoys, by divine institution, supreme, full, immediate, and universal power in the care of souls.' The Papacy is presented as a divinely

↘
✳ The use of the words *Annuntio vobis gaudium magnum: habemus papam*, Latin words meaning: 'We announce with great joy, we have a new Pope' goes back to the days of the election of Martin V in 1417 when three popes claimed the See of Peter. This announcement was given with a sense of relief.

appointed institution that presides over the life of the Church and exercises its rule over God's flock.

Many colourful tourist guides are available to visitors at the Vatican. They highlight all the interesting things that a normal tourist would like to know while walking around the centre of the Roman Catholic Church. But if you really want to know who's who in the Vatican you should get hold of a thick tome: the Pontifical Yearbook. This massive volume of more than 2350 pages contains all sorts of information about everything related to the Vatican and what happens there. Published and updated every year, it faithfully records all events and changes of the previous year. The Pontifical Yearbook is another useful resource for unpacking the theological and institutional significance of the papacy. One particular section lists the official titles of the Pope:

- · 'Bishop of Rome'
- · 'Vicar of Jesus Christ'
- · 'Successor of the prince of the Apostles' (i.e. Peter)
- · 'Supreme Pontiff of the Universal Church'
- · 'Primate of Italy' and 'Archbishop and Metro-politan of the Roman Province'
- · 'Sovereign of the State of the Vatican City'
- · 'Servant of God's servants'.

This list of Papal titles is astonishing and covers various religious offices, political tasks and organizational responsibilities. Each title provides a different perspective on the Papal office, and taken as a whole they help one appreciate who the Pope is and what he does.

BISHOP OF ROME

Another magisterial document that addresses the Pope as Bishop of Rome suggests the following: 'The Shepherd of the Lord's whole flock is the Bishop of the Church of Rome, where the Blessed Apostle Peter, by sovereign disposition of divine Providence, offered to Christ the supreme witness of martyrdom by the shedding of his blood.'[4] The chain of thought that supports such a statement is the following:

- · The apostle Peter was the first Bishop of Rome and was martyred there;
- · the Shepherd of the Church of Rome presides over the 'whole flock';
- · Peter's successors as bishops of Rome are given the same task of shepherding the universal church.

The Pope is the Bishop of Rome in succession to Peter, who is considered the first Bishop and the prototype for all bishops. As Bishop of Rome, he is Pope over the whole church. We will see how this account of Peter and his ministry developed, and how the succession paradigm became the rule for the Roman Catholic Church.

VICAR OF JESUS CHRIST

This title has an important Christological thrust and has been used since the fifth century, although it was in the Middle Ages that it gained wide acceptance over the more

The doctrine of the Threefold Office of Christ (*Triplex munus Christi*)—Jesus Christ being king, prophet and priest—was fully developed by John Calvin. Was it ever meant to apply to a single person in church office?

realistic 'Vicar of Peter'. The Pope is not only the Bishop of Rome (an ecclesiastical claim), but also the one who has represented Christ at the highest human level since His ascension (a Christological claim). The thinking is that the post-resurrection ministry of Jesus Christ needs a human vicar who acts on His behalf until His second coming. In the Roman Catholic understanding all priests act *in persona Christi* (in the person of Christ), but the reference to the Vicar of Christ certainly amplifies its meaning. This title warrants the Papal claims of being a supreme ruler (as Jesus is King), an infallible teacher when he speaks *ex-cathedra* ('from the seat' as Jesus is Prophet), and a high priest in an hierarchical structure (as Jesus is Priest). It therefore tends to blur and confuse what needs to be distinguished, and has been a source of on-going debate within Christianity over the centuries. According to Protestantism, Christ alone (*Solus Christus*) is King, Prophet and Priest in a unique sense. His ministry is a trinitarian work that the Holy Spirit carries out, thus excluding the need for a human 'vicar'.

SUCCESSOR OF THE PRINCE OF THE APOSTLES

This monarchial title needs unpacking to understand what is at stake here. There are two main points: one is the reference to the succession of Peter's office by another bishop, and the other is the attribution to the Apostle Peter of a 'regal' role among the other apostles. The whole structure of the Papacy rests on the idea that Peter ordained his successor as Bishop of Rome, and the pattern of succession continued throughout the centuries. The successors were therefore considered to be in apostolic continuity with the former Bishops of Rome. Here is how the Second Vatican Council (1962–65) puts it: God 'placed blessed Peter over the other apostles, and instituted in him a permanent and visible source and foundation of unity of faith and fellowship.'[5] This 'unbroken' continuity is important for the hierarchical constitution and sacramental structure of the Church of Rome. It is a major argument that Roman Catholics use to distinguish their Church from other Churches (e.g. Protestant and Anglican Churches) which have broken the apostolic chain by separating themselves from Rome.

Protestants also have a concept of unbroken continuity, but it refers to faithfulness to the 'apostolic teaching' of the Church rather than the transmission of the hierarchical outlook of the Church.

SUPREME PONTIFF OF THE UNIVERSAL CHURCH

This title underlines the strong influence of the Roman Imperial structure and offices on the institution of the Papacy. The term pontiff is derived from the Latin word *pontifex*, literally 'bridge builder' (*pons* + *facere*), and indicated a member of the principal college of priests in ancient Rome. The head of the college was known as the *Pontifex Maximus* (the greatest pontiff). Popes have always viewed themselves as the new Pontiff and successor to the Roman imperial structure. In a spiritual sense, the Pope is a bridge builder between God and man and between man and man. *Pontifex Maximum* is seen everywhere in Rome and on Papal buildings and properties in its acronym form (P.M.) as a Papal signature on palaces and monuments. Since the fifteenth century, Popes have liked to refer to themselves using this title, which is still widely used.

PRIMATE OF ITALY AND ARCHBISHOP AND METROPOLITAN OF THE ROMAN PROVINCE

These two titles have an ecclesiastical bearing and a territorial connotation. A Primate is a bishop of the highest rank in a province or country, so the Pope is the primate of Italy and the whole world. Archbishop and Metropolitan are almost synonymous titles and refer to the concrete and territorial role of the Pope as the head of the Church.

SOVEREIGN OF THE STATE OF THE VATICAN CITY

The Pope is a head of state. Though its history may be traced back to the eighth century, the present borders of the Vatican state were defined in 1929 after the Italian army conquered Rome in 1870 making the city the capital of the nation. The Roman Catholic Church is the only church that also has a sovereign state with its own political, financial, juridical and diplomatic structure. It is the only ecclesial body that deals with other states as a state. When the Church signs agreements with another state in the form of a concordat, for instance, it does so according to the rules of international law, as one sovereign country with another. The Pope is head of the church and head of state. When he visits a nation he is welcomed as if he were a king, not simply as an archbishop or some other ecclesiastical figure. Though small and symbolic, the Church also has an army, like any other state. Its double identity (ecclesial and political) is the fruit of its long and complex history, and is also an indication of its composite institutional nature: *both* church *and* state in one. Theology and politics are so intertwined in the system of the Roman Catholic Church and its activities that it is impossible to separate them. The Pope is therefore a religious and a political figure.

It was through an artillery-opened breach in the Roman wall - known as the "Porta Pia breach" - that on September 20, 1870, the Italian soldiers entered Rome and completed the unification of Italy.

SERVANT OF GOD'S SERVANTS

This is the only title that underlines humility and service. It counterbalances the absolute claims and prerogatives of the other titles. In the Gospel of John we read these words of Jesus: 'If I then, your Lord and Teacher, have washed your feet, you also ought to wash one another's feet' (John 13:14). The Pope and all priests, therefore, look to fulfil Christ's injunction to serve the people of God. As the Pope is the Prince of the Apostles, however, he is likewise the Servant of the Servants. Pope Gregory I (590–604) was the first to use this extensively as a papal title, reportedly as a lesson in humility for the Patriarch of Constantinople who had assumed the title 'Ecumenical Patriarch'. Against the background of the other titles, largely shaped by an imperial culture, this one runs the risk of being overtly rhetorical and somewhat overstated.

THE SYMBOLS OF THE PAPACY

Roman Catholicism is a sensual faith. Rather than being based on the discipline of hearing the spoken word, it gives much more attention to visual, olfactory, gestural, ritual and aesthetic dimensions of human life. This is why it has developed such a rich and complex system of symbols for all its actions. This is why liturgy is more important than preaching and sacraments more central than words. The very definition of 'sacrament,'[6] which is paramount for the Roman Catholic faith, with its emphasis on it being a 'sign', 'visible' and part of a 'celebration', witnesses to the 'sensuality' of the Roman Catholic worldview.

The Papacy is no exception. More than any other Western institution it has forged a cluster of symbols to represent its ministry and to express its power even beyond the spiritual and liturgical realms.[7] The process was slow but steady and reached its peak under Pope Innocent III (1198–1216) who implemented the full range of Papal symbolism that marks Popes to this day.

(?) **In the Roman Catholic view, the whole of reality is 'sacramental' in that it witnesses to the visible presence of grace in nature. Why does this tend to underplay the radical effects of sin and to establish a continuity between nature and grace?**

Popes hold the seat of Peter (*cathedra Petri*) which can be seen in the Vatican Basilica. It is a seat that tradition says belonged to Peter himself. It symbolizes the reigning Pope's connection with the teaching and ruling authority of the apostle Peter. Historically, however, the seat displayed in St. Peter's is the throne that Charles the Bald donated to Pope John VIII after his coronation in 875. It is therefore an imperial throne that conveys the fullness of the power of the Pope (*plenitudo potestatis*). A cathedral is a Christian church which contains the seat (*cathedra*) of a bishop, but the Pope's seat is far more important than any other seat. The First Vatican Council in 1870 issued the dogma of Papal infallibility, which established the infallibility of the Pope's teaching when he speaks *ex-cathedra* (from the seat of Peter).

Popes also hold the 'keys' of Peter. Since the fifth century the keys have become symbols of the authority conferred to Peter by Jesus. This is according to a disputed interpretation of Matthew 16:19. It was in the thirteenth century, under the rule of Pope Boniface VIII, that Popes began to be represented holding two keys: one for the heavenly kingdom and one for the earthly kingdom. The keys are also the prominent symbols in the Vatican flag.

From the imperial symbolism of power, the Popes

have inherited the papal tiara—a high cap surrounded by three crowns. The tiara bears a globe surmounted by a cross that the Pope wears during certain ceremonies, and which symbolizes his authority. The three crowns signify the threefold power of the Pope as the 'Father of Kings', 'Rector of the World', and 'Vicar of Christ'. Historically the Popes have thought of themselves as being 'emperors', therefore their reign is analogous to that of political kingdoms with thrones, coronation ceremonies, and royal courts. While it is true that since Paul VI (1963–78) Popes have stopped wearing the tiara and have preferred wearing a more modest miter (a type of headgear), the tiara is still present in the Vatican's coat of arms and flag.

The Popes' clothing is also full of imperial and religious symbolism. The red mantle recalls the one used by Roman and Byzantine emperors. The *pallium* (a woolen cloak) is a vestment that emperors gave to high dignitaries. Popes were among those who inherited these vestments and have thus always worn them. The red in the Pope's clothing also symbolizes the blood of Christ and the martyrs whereas, the white symbolizes the resurrection. Yet, one has to bear in mind that Byzantine emperors also wore white clothes as a sign of purity and nobility.

The language of symbols speaks about the identity of the Papacy as an 'imperial' figure. It is true that twentieth century Popes have gradually shifted to a more sober, less striking exercise of the role of the Papacy. Yet, none of the symbols has been abandoned and at various levels they continue to qualify the Papal office in the modern world.

2

YOU ARE PETER

TU ES PETRUS

THE BIBLICAL BASIS FOR THE PAPACY?

We can view the Papacy from several different angles, all of which offer interesting perspectives. The historical approach sheds light on the intricate developments of a millennial institution that encompasses ancient history and the contemporary world. The political perspective examines the processes through which this religious movement became a political organization, along with all its power structures. Sociological analysis helps us come to terms with the cultural contexts that have shaped the canonical procedures and behavioural patterns of the Papacy. Biographical sketches of individual Popes are excellent sources that offer intriguing and entertaining glimpses into their lives.

All these elements are useful windows into the world of the Papacy, yet none of them are conclusive for a Christian analysis. In fact, foundational to them all is this question: to what extent can the papacy as an institution be traced back to the Bible? In other words, paramount to a Christian study of the Papacy is the testing of its Biblical foundation.[8] After all, the doctrine and the reality of the Papacy appear to be quintessential in defining an important segment of historical and global Christianity— Roman Catholicism. So it is fitting to begin our journey by looking at the Biblical interpretations that allowed the institution of the Papacy to become what it is.

The Papacy is strongly tied to the person and the ministry of Peter. Not only is the Pope thought of as the 'Successor of the Prince of the Apostles', but his ministry is often called the 'petrine' ministry, that is, the governing role attributed to Peter, and by analogy to his successor. Therefore, Peter and his role are of crucial importance in defining the person and the office of the Pope. But what does the Bible say about this?

THE BIBLICAL PETER: A 'PAPAL' PORTRAYAL?

There is no question that Peter is a very important figure in the New Testament.[9] His name occurs 154 times, especially in the Gospels and in Acts. Its Aramaic form, Cephas, is used nine times, mostly in John's Gospel and the Pauline letters to the Galatians and the Corinthians. He is central in much of the early history of the church, from the beginning of Jesus' public ministry (e.g. Mark 1:16–18), to the Lord's appearances after his resurrection (1 Cor. 15:5). The Gospel of John recalls the dialogue between the risen Christ and his perplexed friend (John 21:13–23) after Peter had betrayed him. Peter is among the leaders of the church in the first stages of its existence in Jerusalem (Acts 1:13). He boldly preaches the Gospel to a crowd on the Day of Pentecost (Acts 2:14–41), and again in front of an inquisitive and threatening Sanhedrin (Acts 4–5). Arrested by King Herod because of his continued witness (Acts 12:1–5), he is released from jail miraculously (Acts 12:6–19), and after receiving a vision from God, reaches out to Cornelius, the first Pagan convert to the Christian faith (Acts 10). He is among the influential men that preside over the council of Jerusalem and plays a leading role in shaping its decisions (Acts 15). All in all, Peter is a central figure in the Christian faith.

The New Testament picture of Peter is nonetheless realistic, not idealistic. Peter has strong reservations about his Master's words. Jesus rebukes him because he does not accept that the Messiah should suffer and die (Matt. 16:23). He betrays Jesus in one of his lowest moments during the passion (Luke 22:54–62) and Paul reproaches him because of his hypocritical behaviour concerning the tensions between Jewish and Gentile Christians (Gal. 2:11–16). Moreover, after Acts 15 Peter disappears from Luke's account as the attention shifts to Paul's mission to the Gentiles. The New Testament is not interested in telling the story of Peter's death, apart from a vague prophecy by Jesus concerning Peter's last days (John 21:19). Nothing is said about when, where and under what circumstances Peter died.

The "Crucifixion of Saint Peter" (1600) is a painting by Caravaggio that depicts the martyrdom of Peter by crucifixion. According to tradition, Peter asked that his cross be inverted so as not to imitate his God, Jesus Christ, hence he is depicted upside-down.

Considering all the evidence, the New Testament does not give us an 'hagiographical' account of Peter, as if he were a 'hero' in the way that subsequent traditions have portrayed him in the 'lives of the saints' or in the classical tradition depicting pagan heroes. Peter is a sinner chosen and saved by Jesus. He responds in faith and trusts his Lord, leading with others the early church and always struggling with his doubts and sins.

The New Testament is absolutely clear in recognising the centrality of Jesus Christ in forming, shaping, and heading the church, and also the role of the Holy Spirit. It readily accounts for the strategic function of people such as Peter, among many others, in being part of the community of believers of which the Risen Christ is head and in which the Holy Spirit dwells. Peter was a prominent apostle, but that had little to do with the papal role that would be attributed to him in later centuries. He was a witness among witnesses. He is an elder among elders, and just as important as other sinners saved by

God's grace. In other words, Peter is not the first Pope, nor the 'ideal type' of the Pope.

PETER, THE ROCK AND THE KEYS:
THE CRUX OF THE MATTER

The Biblical witness reflects a sober account of Peter, his person and his role in the early church. He is not unique as a Christian or as a leader, yet he is no mere number in the community of Christ's disciples. Peter represents well the dynamics, the ups and downs, the challenges and opportunities in the spiritual life of a disciple of Christ living in the Christian community. Peter does not stand at the top of a hierarchical organization, nor does the organization have a monarchical role. He is a leader among leaders, he is a disciple among disciples. The question, therefore, is where does the Bible support the understanding of Peter serving and fulfilling a papal role?

The most apparent and quoted evidence are the well-known words of Christ to his servant: 'You are Peter and on this rock I will build my church' (Matt. 16:18). This is deemed to be the cornerstone of the Biblical doctrine of the Papacy, and is the foundation of the doctrinal and ecclesiastical development that shaped the Papacy as we now know it. These words appear inside St. Peter's basilica in a marvellous mosaic, right where the Pope exercises his office.

The interpretation of this passage has been hotly debated for centuries and its meaning is a matter of on-going debate among informed readers of the Bible.[10]

Some critical commentators argue that the Petrine party in the early church inserted this speech by Jesus to support Peter's role and leadership over the Pauline party and the Jacobite party. The background to this hypothesis refers to the argument between Paul and Peter in Galatians 2:11–21, and Paul's recognition of the existence of factions in the Corinthian church mentioned after the names of the apostles (1 Cor. 1:11–12).[11] This view, however, imposes on the canonical Bible a power struggle between the early church leaders. The early church was certainly characterized by various tensions in the inner circle of believers, but they did not reach the point of using apostolic writings as weapons to fight one another.

The standard Roman Catholic interpretation sees in this passage the embryonic stage of the doctrine of the papacy that was later developed into its full form. In it Jesus gives Peter (and by implication his successors) a foundational role in the building of His Church. Subsequent traditions and practices continued to develop

The papacy is an example of how the 'development of doctrine' has been worked out in Roman Catholicism since the post-Constantinian period. The elaboration or development of doctrine is deemed to be the outworking by tradition of what is implicit in Scripture. John Henry Newman strongly advocated this view in his 1845 book *An Essay on the Development of Christian Doctrine*. According to this view, the biblical text implicitly recognizes in Peter what was fully understood later—the Papal office. This understanding of the development of doctrine, however, fails to account for the finality of Scripture—the truth that the Bible is special divine revelation, needing no further revelation. It confuses the illumination of the Spirit in the interpretation of Scripture with the idea of on-going revelation through the magisterium of the Church.

this role to the point at which the papacy eventually emerged. It is difficult, however, to see an organic connection between what the text says and the function of the papacy, with its succession of the Petrine ministry to future generations, with the fundamental importance attributed to the See of Rome, and with the imperial form that the Papacy took. Jesus does not mention or even imply any of these characteristics.

All three Synoptic Gospels report Peter's confession, which precedes what Jesus says to him in Matthew 16, and comes in the context of Jesus announcing his passion, his instructions to his disciples, and the Transfiguration (Matt. 16:13–17:23; Mark 8:19–9:33; Luke 9:18–45).[12] Only Matthew's gospel, however, adds to this discourse the words: 'Tu es Petrus ...'. The context is Jesus' approaching death, a necessary step towards the fulfilment of the Messiah's mission as Saviour and Lord. As He is nearing his death, Jesus asks his disciples who the people say He is, and after that, who they believe Him to be. At this point, Peter pronounces his perhaps most famous words: 'You are the Christ, the Son of the Living God'. These words, however, do not originate from Peter. Jesus promptly replies that they come from a revelation of God. There is nothing inherently Petrine in Peter's confession of faith. It is God who has revealed it and Peter has spoken it. The church (ekklesia), the community of Jesus' disciples, will be built upon the truth (the rock) that Jesus is the Christ, the Son of the Living God. Jesus underlines the fact that 'my' church will be built in such a way. It is not the Petrine church, it is the church founded by Jesus the Messiah.

'I will build my church', says Jesus. Jesus Christ is the Founder and the Builder of the Church, whereas Peter is a witness, a special spokesperson of this divine truth that God revealed to him. Moreover, there is no indication that Peter will have successors to take his place. It is Jesus Christ that will build his church, not Peter or someone else after him.

In amplifying Peter's confession, Jesus says that He will give Peter the keys of the kingdom (16:19). The symbolic significance of the keys has been important for the identity of the Papacy, especially as far as his authority is concerned. The Pope is thought of as being the one who has the power of holding the keys of the church and exercising supreme control over it. In popular imagery, Peter is pictured as the one standing at the gate of heaven opening or closing its door. It is important, however, that the 'keys' Jesus refers to are put in the right Biblical context. In mentioning them, Jesus is quoting Isaiah 22:22 where Shebna, King Hezekiah's steward, is about to be replaced by Eliakim, upon whose shoulder the key of the house of David will be placed. Opening and closing doors with keys is the subordinate role of the steward on behalf of his king. It is not a self-referential, absolute power. It is not something that the steward can do as if he were the king. So, by receiving the keys of the kingdom, Peter will be a servant of God the King who will use him as a steward of the church that Jesus will build. 'Binding and loosing' is another expression that Jesus uses to define what Peter will be called to do (16:19). This is a Jewish saying implying the exercise of discernment (e.g. forbidding and permitting) that leads to decision. In fact, Peter will be part of various decision-making processes in the church's development that will impact the life of the community of Jesus.

As the narrative continues, Jesus announces his imminent passion and death. Peter replies according to his 'flesh and blood' and rebukes Jesus for doing so (16:22). Apparently Peter does not possess infallibility, nor does he exercise a divinely appointed role that is beyond the need for on-going spiritual reformation. Jesus calls Peter 'satan', one whose mind is not on the 'things of God' but on the 'things of men' (16:23). These words shed light on the whole passage, especially if it is interpreted as supporting a papal portrayal of Peter. Peter is safe when he follows the revelation of God and lives under His authority. Peter is utterly unsafe when he acts according to his own understanding and wants to prevail over God's will. The point is that he is not given a leadership role beyond his spirituality. He is not given an office detached from the condition of his heart. He is not assigned a divine office that puts him on a different level to other Christian leaders. Peter is, and remains, a saved sinner that God will use for his purposes in as much as he hears the Word of God and obeys it. Matthew 16 can be seen as the Biblical basis for the Papacy only if the doctrine of the Papacy has already been established apart from Scripture and then subsequently and retrospectively squeezed into it. It is perhaps fair to say that the Papacy created the papal implications of the 'Tu es Petrus …', not the other way around.

'FEED MY SHEEP': THE PAPAL TASK?

From the Roman Catholic perspective, the Biblical evidence for the Papacy has another foundational text which is often presented as establishing the 'nurturing' responsibility of Peter to the church. It is the post-resurrection encounter between Jesus and Peter recorded in John 21:15–23.[13] Apart from the Synoptic Gospels, even John recounts the story of Peter's three denials of Jesus as he was approaching death (John 18). This was perhaps the lowest moment in Peter's life. After the resurrection, however, Jesus restores Peter in a moving conversation that focuses on love and loving Him. 'Do you love me?' asks Jesus three times. After Peter answers each time in the affirmative, Jesus commands him to feed His sheep, to shepherd God's flock, the church (19:17).

The image of God as a shepherd and the people of God as his flock is well established in the Old Testament (e.g. Ps. 23), and Jesus used it in his teaching (e.g. John 10). It also describes the relationship between leaders and the people under their care (e.g. Ezek. 34). After Peter confirms his faithfulness to his Risen Lord, Jesus, instead of forsaking him, applies this imagery to Peter and commands him to 'feed the sheep'. Feeding the flock, caring for the church, and being servant leaders of God's people is the standard task of every shepherd of the church. In church life, every pastor is called to feed, protect, nurture, and keep together the people of God entrusted to him. Peter himself confirms this to his fellow-elders (1 Peter 5:2), but does not advocate a unique office for himself. In Jesus' commission there is no indication of an exclusive or superior responsibility set aside for Peter, nor is there implied a hierarchical structure of which Peter is the head. As with Matthew 16, the doctrine of the Papacy can be envisaged in John 21 only if it has already been established elsewhere and then retrospectively traced back to this Gospel text.

In the words of a present-day Roman Catholic theologian, 'the Catholic Church remains convinced that the Petrine office is a permanent part of its divine constitution. The New Testament uses three images to describe the ministry which Christ entrusted to Peter and through him to his successors. It calls him rock, the church's firm foundation. It says he has the keys of God's house, to keep out intruders and foreign elements. And it portrays him as the shepherd, charged to feed the flock and ward off dangers.'[14] As has been demonstrated, these claims about what the New Testament says about Peter and his ministry are dubious, if not altogether wrong. The 'rock' certainly does not refer to Peter, nor are his successors envisaged here. The 'keys' do have a ministerial role in the service of the church, but nothing of a magisterial and absolute power in the name of Christ. The 'shepherd' image is not in any sense exclusive to Peter, but defines all those who are called to be servant leaders of the church.

FIRST PETER AS THE FIRST ENCYCLICAL?

Claims for a biblical background to the Papacy, focus mainly on these two passages, neither of which provide a solid biblical foundation. This is, to say the least, problematic considering its doctrinal importance. A recent lecture by Pope Benedict XVI (now emeritus) to a group of seminarians in Rome on February 8, 2013 offers a summary of the main Roman Catholic arguments regarding Peter and the Papacy. This was not his last speech as Pope, but it was his last theological discourse prior to his resignation. In a certain sense this *lectio* offers insight into his way of thinking and interpreting Scripture. The text of the discourse was 1 Peter 1:3–5, a dense text full of theological richness. Benedict XVI applied all of his catechetical skills to expounding it. His comments were profound, as one might expect from a significant theologian, yet revealing of his particular Roman Catholic blend of Biblical teaching.

In introducing the letter, Ratzinger said it was the 'first encyclical' the Vicar of Christ sent to the Church. Let's consider this for a moment. An encyclical is, generally speaking, a circulating letter, but technically speaking it is a letter sent by the Roman Catholic Pope to bishops, clergy, the faithful, and the people of good will of his time concerning doctrinal and pastoral issues.

Since the 1740s, Popes have regularly sent encyclicals. At the very least it is not historically appropriate to give 1 Peter a papal term that would not be put into use for another 1,700 years. Even if we take the more general meaning of encyclical (i.e. a circulating letter), 1 Peter is not the first NT text of the canon in terms of the chronology of its composition. Paul's first letter to the Thessalonians is the earliest New Testament document.

So, even if the adjective 'first' refers to the chronological priority of Peter's letter, this is not the case in that other apostolic letters were written before Peter's first epistle.

Beyond historical details, the message that Benedict wanted to convey was that of an on-going continuity between Peter writing his letter and future Popes writing their encyclicals. The Pope linked this Biblical letter to modern encyclicals and Peter to modern Popes. This claim is hermeneutically loaded with the Roman Catholic understanding of Peter's office and succession, but does not stand out from the text of Scripture itself.

It is not by chance that in his *lectio* Benedict XVI mentions Peter as the 'Vicar of Christ'. After rightly recalling the way in which Peter introduces himself as an 'apostle', he goes on to say that Peter was commissioned to be 'the first apostle, the Vicar of Christ'. He makes the case that Peter wrote from Rome (the Babylon quoted in 5:13), and that his being in Rome carries with it theological significance. As Vicar of Christ, and in view of his universal office, Peter had to preside over the Jewish church in Jerusalem first, and eventually over the Gentile church in Rome.

The 'vicar' title does not come from Peter himself. The apostle rather talks of himself as an 'elder' (5:1) in the company of other elders, thus a fellow-elder. There is no hint in the text that Peter has received the title of 'vicar', whatever the term may mean. Peter does not think of himself as someone or something that his fellow-elders are not. Moreover, he calls the whole people of God 'a chosen people, a royal priesthood, a holy nation' called to declare the praises of God (2:9). Peter's definition of Rome as Babylon may have apocalyptic significance, rather than being a reference to the beginning of a universal Papacy. Again, Ratzinger's interpretation is loaded with meanings that belong to the Roman Catholic tradition, but cannot be found in Scripture.

There is much wisdom in Benedict's last *lectio* on 1 Peter. Yet it is wisdom driven by certain Roman Catholic presuppositions that govern his reading rather than by Scripture itself. The same could be said about the extensive literature that portrays the Bible as supporting the doctrine of the Papacy as something stemming from *ius divinum* (i.e. divine law). On the contrary, this doctrine cannot be found in Scripture in the way it is articulated in the Roman Catholic tradition. One needs to look elsewhere, to the subsequent history of the church and the development of dogma to find its present-day forms. To this end, we now turn to look at the long historical process that led to the shaping of the Papacy as we now know it.

Every reader of the Bible risks doing "eisegesis" instead of "exegesis". While the latter means gathering the meaning "out" of the text, the former means putting a predetermined meaning 'into' it. Pre-understanding in interpretation is inevitable, but the text should always be given priority over the reader's presuppositions.

3

HEAD OF THE CHURCH

CAPUT ECCLESIAE

THE HISTORICAL DEVELOPMENT
OF THE PAPACY UP TO THE RENAISSANCE

It is impossible to establish from the Bible alone any idea that fairly resembles the Papacy as advocated by Roman Catholicism. The Bible records that Peter had a leadership role in the early church but does not portray Peter as having hierarchical primacy over the other apostles. The New Testament witnesses to Peter's involvment in consolidating the church, but does not contain a doctrine of apostolic succession where Peter would have successors as monarchs do. The Bible does not directly link the person and the ministry of Peter to the city of Rome as if this relationship should carry any theological significance. It altogether omits to tell us what actually happened to Peter in the last days of his life. On the whole, the witness of Scripture does not fit the role, the office and the power that is attributed to the Roman Pope. Trying to square biblical teaching with the reality of the Papacy is more of an *a posteriori* theological attempt than something that springs from Scripture. To understand what driving forces contributed to the growth in importance of the Papal office, one has to look at historical developments in the first centuries of the Church.

THE BEGINNINGS OF THE PAPACY

One fundamental factor behind the creation of the papacy, is Peter's presence and martyrdom in Rome. As we have seen, the Bible is silent on this matter. Historical sources and archaeological evidence are somewhat dubious about both issues, but what is certain is that the tradition that Peter was martyred in Rome and his body was buried in a cemetery area on the Vatican hill gained immediate and widespread acceptance. This story about the end of Peter's life, coupled with a similar account about Paul,

In Romans chapter 16 many people and names are referred to but Peter is never mentioned. If this silence is due to the fact that Peter went to Rome after Paul's letter had been written, then the argument that Peter "founded" the church of Rome totally collapses. The church in Rome had already been founded before Peter and Paul.

soon caused Rome to be considered as the city where
Peter and Paul were martyred, and the church of Rome as
the Christian community that was led by both apostles.
Rome began to be surrounded by an apostolic 'aura' and
a sense of high respect because of Peter and Paul. The
possible burial place of Peter soon became the object of
pilgrimages and religious meetings. When the Emperor
Constantine (274–337 AD) decided to build churches in
Rome, the Vatican hill was an obvious place to begin.
When the exact location and disposition of the church
was discussed, the idea of having the altar right above
the imagined place of Peter's tomb guided the decision.

The identification between Peter and Rome, between
Peter and the church of Rome, between Peter and the
place where he died, began to solidify more and more.
A whole tradition emerged around the association of
Peter and Rome. Another strand of thought pushed
the identification even further. After Peter's death, the
leaders of the church of Rome began to be respected
and honored as his 'successors' and clothed with the
'apostolic' authority of Peter. Rome became the special
'see' that had seen Peter and Paul as the leaders of church.
While the title of 'bishop' hardened its meaning and was
put in a hierarchical framework of church government,
the see of Rome and the bishops that came after Peter
were increasingly seen as a special church and as special
leaders. Ignatius of Antioch (ca 50–117) began to refer to
the Church of Rome as the Church 'which presides in
charity',[15] although this presidency stems from Christian
fellowship, it is spiritual in nature and exercised in love.

Much of the development did not happen in a vacuum, but in the context of rising doctrinal and pastoral controversies. Irenaeus (c. 130–202), bishop of Lyon, in confronting the heresy of Gnosticism, argued that the true apostolic doctrine could be found with the bishops that had been instituted by the apostles and their successors. According to Irenaeus, this was particularly true as far as Rome was concerned. Each church should have agreed with the church of Rome because—as Irenaeus erroneously believed—this church had been founded by Peter and Paul and had kept the apostolic tradition.[16] For this reason, he compiled a list of bishops of Rome to show the continuity between the two apostles and their successors and to underline the importance of being in agreement with the church of Rome. Still at this point there is no indication of a properly defined doctrine of the primacy of the see of Rome and its bishop over the whole church. Irenaeus' argument, not unlike that of Cyprian of Carthage (c. 200–258), is driven mainly by apologetical concerns and is an attempt to find loose institutional criteria to establish the orthodox doctrine in the midst of theological debates.

THE POPE AS EMPEROR

The Papacy would have never emerged if there was no Empire forming the political and cultural *milieu* of the life of the early church. The slow process that led to the formation of the Papacy depended on the importance of Rome as the capital city of the Empire and the power it exercised in the ancient world. The ideology of the *Roma aeterna* (eternal Rome) crept into the church and influenced the way that Christians thought about the role of the church of Rome, seeing an analogy with the role of the city in the affairs of the empire.

From the fourth century onwards, the bishops of Rome, for example Damasus I (366–84) and Siricius (384–99) claimed to be the successors of the apostle Peter and in their understanding this made them mediators in controversies or judges of various conflicts. What was a bottom-up, spiritual, and brotherly recognition of an apostolic descent of the church of Rome, turned into a top-down, authoritative, and legal claim of the same church over the other churches. The right to appeal to Rome in the Roman Empire also became an ecclesiastical pattern as far as church affairs were concerned. What began as advice and counsel sought from the bishops of Rome was turned into directives and orders. The denomination of the *sedes apostolica* (apostolic see) which earlier referred to all the churches that had been founded by the apostles, began to indicate the church of Rome alone, and with legally binding overtones. The concept of Rome exercising 'primacy' took shape and the right of the bishop of Rome to rule beyond the Roman church was established. The bishop of Rome, though holding an equal office to other bishops, was considered as superior due to his privilege of being head of the most important apostolic see. It is at this point that a Biblical text like Matthew 16:18 was interpreted in a 'papal' sense as if it would give Scriptural support to the growing profile of the bishop of Rome. The latter was thought of as continuing the mission of Peter against the background of Roman inheritance law. The whole idea of succession was indebted to the legal patterns of Roman law, which were transposed into the life of the church and into Biblical interpretation. It was Innocent I (402–17) that reinforced the idea of the Papacy as a legally defined office stemming from the bishop of Rome as Peter's successor. If Irenaeus had stressed the importance of Rome as holding to the apostolic tradition—thus referring to a spiritual and doctrinal dimension—Innocent underlined its role based on divine law, resulting in an authoritative office. The assimilation of Roman juridical categories was eventually completed.

This is the context of what happened with the 'Constantinian shift'.[17] After the Edict of Milan had recognized the Christian religion as legitimate in the Roman Empire (313), Constantine the Great became the first Emperor that supported the church and for political reasons became a strong advocate of the hierarchical unity of the church. With gifts and fiscal exemptions, the church acquired strong secular interests in terms of real estate and financial transactions. The 'temporal' interests of the church grew in importance and became prominent in the life of the church. The growing relationship between the church and the Empire caused

✱ Though very influential in church affairs, even summoning the Council of Nicea in 325, Emperor Constantine (272–337) was only baptized as a Christian as he approached death in 337 by the Arianizing bishop Eusebius of Nicomedia.

their organisational differences to be less and less visible. A *do ut des* (i.e. exchange of favors) culture characterized the cooperation between the two. Subsequent secular claims by Popes made extensive use of the so-called *Donation of Constantine* (*donatio Constantini*). This is a forged Roman imperial decree by which the emperor Constantine supposedly transferred authority over Rome and the western Empire to the Pope. The document was fake. Composed probably in the eighth century, it was used, especially in the Middle Ages, in support of the papacy's claims of political authority. It was Lorenzo Valla (1405–57), an Italian priest and Renaissance humanist, who is credited with first exposing the forgery with philological arguments in the fifteenth century.

The early church in Rome was formed by different Christian communities gathered in homes and forming a network of organically-related churches. After Constantine, the church became more structured and hierarchical, following the pattern of the existing political Empire. As the Roman Empire gradually abandoned the West, what was left in Rome was the 'imperial' structure of the church with the pope as its head. It was between the fourth and the fifth century that Popes applied to themselves the imperial title of Pontifex.

THE HARDENING OF PAPAL PRIMACY

The climax of this long process of the bishop of Rome becoming an emperor-type leader and the church of Rome becoming an empire-type organization culminated with Pope Leo I (440–61). At this time, Rome as *caput Imperii* (head of the Empire) became interchangeable with Rome *caput Ecclesiae* (head of the Church). The Papacy as a fully-orbed institution became a properly defined theory.

Leo extended the primacy of the bishop of Rome from doctrinal issues only to the wider leadership of the church. He insisted on using the title 'vicar of Christ'. As Peter was the vicar of Christ, so the pope, having succeeded Peter as bishop of Rome, is the vicar of Christ. The conceptual framework for such a syllogism was taken from Roman law and applied to Scripture to find proofs for it. Assuming that Jesus had given Peter full power (*potentia*) and had elevated him to be the head (*princeps*) of the church, Leo was convinced that the bishop of Rome as Peter's successor had full power to intervene in all churches over essential issues of doctrine and Christian life, even beyond or independently of synods.

The consolidation process of the Papacy was also tempered by more nuanced views than those of Leo. Pope Gregory I (590-604) introduced the title *Servus Servorum Dei* (servant of the servants of God), but as a further expansion of the names of the Pope rather than a question mark over the 'imperial' ones. It is not by chance that Leo and Gregory, and they alone in the long history of the Papacy, received the appellative *Magnum* (great) to indicate the high recognition that they had both received.

As the capital of the Roman empire changed from Rome to Constantinople—the New Rome—the power of the Roman Pope on the western hemisphere became even more 'political' given that the only powerful institution left in Rome was the church. After the fall of the Western Roman Empire (476), the Pope acted as if he were the new Emperor.[18] The more formally defined and binding jurisdiction of the Pope was one reason that the Eastern church became more and more distant from the Western church to the point of breaking with it in the famous Schism (1054).

The reference to the 'second Rome' stemmed from the idea that Constantinople was the successor to the legacy of ancient Rome, the 'first Rome'. After the fall of Constantinople under the Ottoman Empire (1493), the name of 'third Rome' was given to Moscow whereas the claimed successors of the Western Roman Empire such as the Papal States or the Holy Roman Empire claimed to be the 'second Rome'.

Another development worth considering is the refinement of the doctrine of the 'two swords' and the 'two kingdoms'. Leo I was again influential in this respect. In fact, he wanted close cooperation between church and state, while maintaining the autonomy of each sphere. They were two powers, i.e. the *potestas imperialis* (imperial power) and the *auctoritas sacerdotalis* (priestly authority). The same basic view was held by important Fathers like Ambrose of Milan (337–97) and Augustine of Hippo (354–430). It is also true that according to Leo the Great the priority always lay with the religious authority. The relationship between the two powers has always been an on-going source of debate and controversy and this arrangement was not the last word on the issue. The scene of Charlemagne being crowned as Emperor by Pope

Leo III on Christmas Day 800 portrays the relationship between the two 'swords' whereby the spiritual sword supports and legitimizes the temporal, and the temporal sword submits to and serves the spiritual. The alliance brought about the secularization of the spiritual authority and the sacralization of the political power. Both parties however always wanted to use and abuse each other. Pope Nicholas I (858–67) claimed to have *plenitudo potestatis* (full power) over the whole church, monarchs included. On their part, emperors like Otto the Great (936–73) claimed to have a voice in the election of the Pope and bishops, thus suggesting that the secular power should influence the church.

As the 800 crowning celebration of Charlemagne took place, the relationship between the Pope, who was crowning the Emperor in Europe, and the Eastern church, which was faithful to the Emperor in Constantinople, was further weakened. Innocent III (1198–1216) overloaded the title *vicarius Christi* (vicar of Christ) to the point of asserting the pope's supremacy over any human being. He also claimed the right to assess the worthiness of the elected Emperor. In 1216 the same Pope approved the order of Francis of Assisi who had asked to live in poverty. Evidently, it was all right for the Pope to authorize Francis to do that as Francis had not challenged the power structure of the church. On the theological side, Thomas Aquinas (1245–74) tried to moderate these claims by arguing that the Church had only an indirect power over secular affairs (*potestas indirect in temporalibus*).

Perhaps the clearest example of an imperial Pope is Boniface VIII (1235–1303). He put forward some of the strongest claims to temporal and spiritual power of any Pope and constantly involved himself with foreign affairs. In his Bull of 1302, *Unam Sanctam*, Boniface VIII proclaimed that the Pope has full, unlimited and direct power over kings. Since he holds the 'two swords', the spiritual and the temporal, the Bull pushed papal supremacy to its historical extreme. These views, and his chronic intervention in 'temporal' affairs, led to many bitter quarrels with the powerful of his day, that is, Emperor Albert I of Habsburg and King Philip IV of France. The famous Italian poet Dante Alighieri wrote his essay *De Monarchia* to dispute Boniface's claims of papal supremacy. Prior to Boniface VIII, Pope Leo IX (1049–54), the one under whom the Eastern Schism occurred, spoke of the church of Rome as *caput* (head), *mater* (mother), *fons* (source, origin), and *fundamentum* (foundation) of the whole church.

Writing in 1148 to Pope Eugene II, Bernard of Clairvaux (1090–1153) summarized common views of the Papal office in the Middle Ages: 'Who are you? The high priest, the Supreme Pontiff. You are the prince of the bishops, you

On February 22, 1300, Boniface VIII published the Bull *Antiquorum fida relatio*, in which, appealing vaguely to the precedent of past ages, he declares that he grants afresh and renews certain 'great remissions and indulgences for sins' which are to be obtained 'by visiting the city of Rome and the venerable basilica of the Prince of the Apostles'. The long trajectory of the practice of indulgences that eventually led to the sixteenth century Protestant Reformation started there.

are the heir of the Apostles; in primacy you are Abel, in governing you are Noah, in patriarchate you are Abraham, in orders you are Melchizedek, in dignity you are Aaron, in authority you are Moses, in judgment you are Samuel, in power you are Peter, by anointing, you are Christ. You are the one to whom the keys have been given, to whom the sheep have been entrusted' (*De Consideratione*).

Going back to Innocent III, it is worth noting that during his reign the Papal state reached its greatest extension in central Italy. Private and public gifts from the fourth century onwards had enriched the church, but it was when the Frankish kings donated duchies and provinces that the Papal possessions became a 'state', a distinct territory under Papal rule. The head of the church became also the head of a state, the 'Papal Prince'.[19]

The gradual assimilation of imperial categories transformed the Papacy into yet another European monarchy with universal claims. Though significantly smaller than its early modern borders, the Vatican State still exists today and it allows the Pope to claim the title of 'Sovereign of the State of the Vatican City'. The combination between religious and political claims continues to define the Papal office. This is an example of how the papacy is more a child of its history than a leadership structure strictly defined by Biblical categories.

POPES AND ANTIPOPES

Although the Papacy is considered as the visible bond of unity of the church, there was a long period in history in which rival contenders for the office of the Pope would fight between them to prevail. This time of crisis and confusion was even more complicated by controversies on the relationship between the powers of the Pope and that of church councils. This theological dispute, coupled with general dissatisfaction caused by the scandal of Popes living lustfully and violently, formed the background for the radical questions that were eventually posed by the Protestant Reformation in the sixteenth century.

The period with different competing popes is referred to as the Great Western Schism (1309–1417) or as Martin Luther would call it: the 'Babylonian Captivity of the Church'. The election of rival popes and the removal of the papacy from Rome to Avignon, in southern France, provoked the schism. This was not the first time that Popes had left Rome. In fact, Pope Alexander IV had moved the Papal court to the Italian city of Viterbo (60km from Rome) in 1257 to free it from the influence of Roman noble families on church affairs. It was Pope Martin IV who eventually transferred the Papacy back to Rome in 1281.

Coming back to the Western Schism, here is how Joseph Ratzinger, before becoming Pope Benedict XVI, summarized its gist: 'For nearly half a century, the Church was split into two or three obediences that excommunicated one another, so that every Catholic lived under excommunication by one pope or another, and, in the last analysis, no one could say with certainty which of the contenders had right on his side. The Church no longer offered certainty of salvation; she had become questionable in her whole objective form—the true Church, the true pledge of salvation, had to be sought outside the institution'.[20] In a sense, apart from the already consummated Eastern Schism in 1054, the Western church ceased to be 'one' and 'catholic' long before the Protestant Reformation.

Throughout the Middle Ages, there was constant strife between popes and kings, leading to excommunication from the one and imprisonment by the other. Each party used its own weapon to fight the battle. However, it was the disruption of the papal succession that provoked widespread anxiety within the church. Between 1305 and 1377, the pope was French and so were most of his cardinals. The schism was consummated when the Pope in Rome (Urban VI) and the Pope in Avignon (Clement VII) excommunicated each other. The conflict therefore reached the heart of the church. The division continued because each Pope appointed his own successor, thus propagating and exacerbating the quarrel.

Apart from being theologically disputable, are the Roman Catholic claims for the unbroken continuity of the Papacy historically convincing?

Who would resolve this conflict? Some theologians had argued that church councils always had priority over the pope.[21] The early ecumenical councils were a prime example whereby disputes in the church were addressed and solved in large gatherings of bishops. However, in this case it became clear that councils could take wrong decisions and were part of the problem, rather than the solution. The Council of Pisa (1409), for example, elected a third pope to replace the two rivals. At the Council of Constance (1414–18), where the reformer Jan Hus was condemned to the flames in Prague, the two rival popes and the third pope were replaced now by a fourth one, Martin V. The disruption intensified. The Papacy as an institution was seriously undermined in that the Council declared its sovereignty over the pope. Pope Martin V, who could not attend, declared its position on this matter null. As a binding council for the Church, some Roman Catholic theologians today invoke its memory for a new conciliar movement—a pattern of church government that amplifies the role of councils at the expense of the exclusive claims of an 'imperial' Papacy.

Between the fourteenth and sixteenth centuries, leading theologians enriched the debate. They defended the authority of Scripture over councils, and of councils over the pope, drawing on the example of the ancient church. Advocating the position that Scripture is above the whole church, William of Ockham (d. 1349) argued that the whole church (including laity) should hold a council to elect the pope and limit his authority. Ockham's view had an ecclesiological thrust in that he believed that this whole church is the communion of saints (of all saints), not the Roman church in its hierarchical sense. The outcome of such an argument is evident: if a pope falls into heresy, a council can judge him without asking permission and without his approval. Marsilius of Padua agreed in his major work *Defensor Pacis* (1324):

the church consists of all the faithful, not just priests and those belonging to religious orders. Christ is the only head of the church.

The last gasp of the conciliar movement came at the Council of Basel (1431–49). Papalists formed the Council of Florence, while the conciliar party in Basel elected another pope. Martin called it, but died before it met. Eugenius IV (1431–47) succeeded him and was prevented by ill-health from presiding. He could not have done so in any case, as the fathers declared (on the basis of Constance) that the Council was superior to the pope.

Finally, on the eve of the Reformation, Pope Julius II (1503–13) reasserted papal primacy and packed the Fifth Lateran Council (1512–17) with supportive cardinals.[22] Thomas Cajetan, famous as Martin Luther's curial opponent, staunchly defended papal primacy. In condemning the Reformation, the Council of Trent also condemned positions that theologians well within the pale of the conciliar movement had argued for centuries. These old debates about the relationship between Popes and councils are still part of the discussion with the Roman Catholic Church. The term used to try to overcome both extremes is 'collegiality', so the Pope is the supreme head of the Church but he governs it by involving and calling for the participation of the hierarchy.

WARRIORS AND PATRONS

As the distinction between the Pope as a religious leader and as head of state collapsed, popes interpreted their role as players in world affairs through political and military means. While maintaining an appearance of men devoted to Christian virtues and disciplines within a religious institution, their real concerns were more material than spiritual. Sometimes they acted more like warrior kings than preachers of the Gospel.

Between the eleventh and the sixteenth century, the Crusades are an example of such a totally unwarranted emphasis. A crusade was fought against those perceived to be internal or external enemies of Christendom, be it through the recovery of Christian property or the defense of the interests of the Church.[23] The first crusade was called by Pope Urban II in 1095 with the stated goal of restoring Christian access to the holy places near Jerusalem. Under the banner of the 'cross', thus the name 'crusade', Muslims were the primary enemies of these military campaigns, but there were also crusades, motivated by political and religious reasons, against pagans, heretics, and people under the ban of excommunication. Popes became political facilitators and spiritual fathers of the crusades.

The Popes provided spiritual justification for these military campaigns by elaborating a theology of military conquest, and occupation of the lands that were historically and symbolically important for Christians. They also generated the system of 'plenary indulgences' for the crusaders, that is, the remission of temporal punishment due to sin for those who had responded to the call of joining the crusades. This indulgence system became prominent in the sixteenth century when indulgences were sold to finance important ecclesiastical building projects in Rome. It was Martin Luther that hanged the 95 theses in 1517, which revolved around the theology and practice of indulgences, thus giving rise to the Protestant Reformation. The unsettled memory, emotional scars and political controversies around the crusades are still matters of on-going uneasiness between Christians and Muslims world-wide.

At the turning of the Middle Age into the Modern Era, Popes became part of the new cultural milieu that marked the European scene. The Roman curia, made of Popes and cardinals around them, was not different from other Italian courts of the time. The Renaissance culture, with its fascination for the recovery of classical standards of beauty, and its renewed attention towards the arts, affected papal Rome as everywhere else.[24] The Renaissance Popes strived to transform Rome into the arts capital of the world. Nicholas V (1447–55), the first of them, built sumptuous churches, buildings, fountains and bridges to embellish the city. He was also an insatiable lover of ancients codices and books, thus forming the core collection of the world famous Vatican Library. Under Sixtus IV (1471–84) Rome became a magnificent Renaissance city. The Pope gathered famous painters and is renowned for having given the name to the 'Sistine Chapel' where Michelangelo later painted the Last Judgment fresco. Julius II (1503–13) began rebuilding St. Peter's basilica, gathering in his courts artists of the caliber of Raphael and Michelangelo. These artists provided a figurative representation of the comprehensive vision of Roman Catholicism which embraced classical and Christian cultures. In the magnificent Signature Room, Raphael painted Plato and Aristotle as anticipators of Christian wisdom. In the breathtaking Sistine Chapel, Michelangelo recapitulated the history of the world by interspersing characters of Biblical history and pagan history as a way of saying that the Church inherits both traditions.

The Renaissance painters who decorated the Vatican Palace conveyed the theological vision of the Roman Church of the time. Architects like Gian Lorenzo Bernini (1598–1680) designed the shape of St. Peter's square to indicate the catholicity of the Roman Church whose arms are stretched to embrace the whole world.

The Renaissance Popes were also public and outspoken in their lifestyles which were contrary to Canon law, at least on paper. Sixtus IV had many children and welcomed them into the Vatican. The practice of nepotism—favoring children and relatives in positions of leadership—became the ethos of the Papal court. Innocent VIII (1484–92) went as far as organizing wedding parties for his children and admitting his 13-year-old nephew to the college of cardinals. The negative peak was perhaps reached by Alexander VI (1492–1503), Rodrigo Borgia, whose many illegitimate sons lived in such a corrupt way that the Borgia family became synonymous with ruthless and immoral behavior. It was in such a cultural and spiritual climate that the Protestant Reformation emerged. While Popes concentrated on their artistic and family affairs, the quest for spiritual renewal began in Europe.

From the apostle Peter in Rome in the first century to the Renaissance Papal princes of early modern history is a long journey. Popes have been bishops, theologians, statesmen, warriors, patrons, and saints. The imperial pattern was the influential blueprint that shaped the Papal institution from the fourth and fifth centuries onwards. What began as a position of leadership in the church became a position of power that resembled the secular paradigm of authority. The 'papalizing' reading of the biblical texts on Peter was a later attempt to justify the imperial Papacy biblically and theologically, yet the Papacy is more a child of imperial than biblical categories as its long history up to the sixteenth century Reformation clearly demonstrates.

4

IS THE POPE THE ANTICHRIST?

PROTESTANT ASSESSMENTS OF THE PAPACY

The Papacy has had critics throughout the centuries. It is fair to say, however, that it was the sixteenth century Protestant Reformation that developed the most comprehensive and massive argument against the Papacy, pulling together biblical, doctrinal, historical, moral, and institutional threads. The most brilliant minds of the Reformation engaged in the controversy concerning the Papacy and many major Protestant confessions included an explicit reference to it. Having said that, the Protestant critique reached its peak with the identification of the Pope as the Antichrist. According to the New Testament, the Antichrist is against Christ and His church, wanting to take His place and destroy His work (e.g. 2 Thess. 2). For Christians, the Antichrist is the enemy par excellence. This equation stirred religious emotions more than many subtle theological arguments. One of the most important figures of the Counter-Reformation, cardinal Roberto Bellarmino (1542–1621), acknowledged the consensus of all Protestants that the Pope was the Antichrist when he wrote that 'all heretics of this era teach similar things, especially Luther, Illyricus, Musculus, Beza, Bullinger'.[25]

The Protestant Reformation was not the first movement that referred to the Pope as the Antichrist. A robust Medieval European tradition—from the Waldensians to Wycliffe, and down to the Hussites—had denounced the Pope in such a radical way. This is why a recent Roman Catholic and Lutheran dialogue in the United States acknowledges this fact: 'In calling the pope the "antichrist" the early Lutherans stood in a tradition that reached back into the eleventh century. Not only dissidents and heretics but even saints had called the bishop of Rome the 'antichrist' when they wished to castigate his abuse of power'.[26] What is said here about the Lutherans extends to other Reformation traditions. Even in this case the Reformers were not necessarily innovative but relied on previous, well-attested strands of thought.

LUTHER AND THE APOCALYPTIC ANTICHRIST

Martin Luther and the Pope have long been perceived as representing the two enemies within Western

Christianity. Their persons embodied the religious conflict that took place in the sixteenth century giving rise to the Protestant Reformation and the Counter-Reformation. The expression 'Luther and the Pope' has become 'Luther *or* the Pope', either one or the other.[27] Before Luther rejected the Pope, the Pope had already rejected Luther by condemning him first in 1520 and then excommunicating him in 1521. So it is difficult to establish who first broke fellowship with the other. In fact, before burning the 1520 Papal bull, *Exsurge Domine,* which contained his condemnation, Luther was a devout Roman Catholic and highly esteemed the Pope. His acceptance of the Papacy was totally uncritical. He believed that the problem lay with the curia around the Pope, not with the Pope himself. Even after hanging the *Ninety-Five Theses* in 1517 he had hopes of finding a hearing with the Pope concerning the need to correct certain moral abuses and doctrinal errors. In the *Theses*, Luther is chiefly concerned with limiting the powers of the Pope, not considering them self-referential and unlimited, but instead under Gospel standards (e.g. Thesis 5). For example, Popes have no power over souls in Purgatory, only God does (Theses 22 and 25). Popes cannot give absolution if God

Luther visited Rome in 1511 and was shocked to see the corruption of the Roman clergy. He also began to have doubts about the whole theology and practice of the indulgences in observing what went on at the "Scala Sancta". These Holy Steps were thought of as being the same steps that Jesus had climbed in Jerusalem and were climbed on the knees by pilgrims in order to receive an indulgence.

has not granted it (Thesis 6). Popes can only act within the boundaries set by the Word of God.

At this stage, Luther begins to counter the absolute claims of the primacy of the Pope or of the Councils with the primacy of Scripture. In writing against the Catholic theologian Johannes Eck in 1519, Luther develops his critical approach towards the Papacy with a fuller set of arguments (*Resolutio Lutherana ... de potestate papae*). The authority of Popes and Councils should be subordinate to the Bible. Christ did not institute the Papacy; it was established by the Church in the course of its history. It comes not from 'divine law', but is a human institution. The 'rock' of Matthew 16 is not a reference to Peter, but is his confession of Jesus on behalf of the whole church or Christ himself. He alone is the foundation of the Church. The Roman Popes have nothing 'petrine' about them, nor is there anything 'Papal' in Peter. The Papacy is not commanded or foreseen by Scripture, and therefore obedience to the Word of God must take precedence over obedience to the Pope. If the Pope disobeys Scripture, faithful Christians should follow the latter without hesitation. Christians are not obligated to obey an unfaithful Pope.

Although the debate was becoming hotter, it was only after his definitive excommunication in 1521 that Luther elaborated his even more radical critique of the Papacy. At this point, Luther became convinced that the supreme adversary of the Christian faith was its supreme representative, the Pope. The Papacy had become a power structure and could no longer serve the cause of the gospel, but served instead the carnal interests of the Church. In his response to Ambrogio Caterino (an Italian Dominican monk who had written a defense of the Pope and against Luther on the topic), the German reformer turned his opposition to the Papacy into an apocalyptic argument. In commenting on Daniel 8:23–5, Luther identifies the ferocious king of the passage who devastates the saints as the Pope. Playing with the double meaning of the Greek word *anti*, Luther argues that the Pope is against Christ and takes his place by claiming to act on his behalf. He is a counterfeit Christ. He is therefore the Antichrist. According to Luther, his times were marked by the imminent end of the world; this then demanded that the situation be painted in black and white. The Pope and the Turks were the representatives of the Antichrist and were focusing their final attack on the Church of Christ.

In 1534 Luther drafted the *Smalcald Articles*, which are a summary of Christian doctrine from a Lutheran perspective. In art. 4, Luther speaks of the Pope's power as 'false, mischievous, blasphemous, and arrogant' mainly interested in 'diabolic affairs'. His critique, however, is not confined to his contemporary experience of the Papacy, but draws on historical and theological arguments. In the same article he writes: 'it is manifest that the holy Church has been without the Pope for at least more than five hundred years, and that even to the present day the churches of the Greeks and of many other languages neither have been nor are yet under the Pope. Besides, as often remarked, it is a human figment which is not commanded, and is unnecessary and useless; for the holy Christian [or catholic] Church can exist very well without such a head, and it would certainly have remained better [purer, and its career would have been more prosperous] if such a head had not been raised up by the devil. And the Papacy is also of no use in the Church, because it exercises no Christian office; and therefore it is necessary for the Church to continue and to exist without the Pope'. A church without the Pope captures Luther's vision at this point.

In 1545, one year before dying, Luther wrote his final fierce thoughts on the Papacy. In his work *Against the Papacy at Rome, Founded by the Devil*, he is aware that the final, eschatological hour is at hand. The Pope is a child of the Devil, who wants to destroy the Church through the sword of the Turks and the lies of the Pope. It is an eschatological emergency reaching its final stage. No compromise is possible under these circumstances; evil is to be denounced and fought against relentlessly.

Luther's views of the Papacy developed over his life from initial acceptance to total rejection. His apocalyptic views shed a sinister light on the Pope and shaped his harsh language against him. Yet Luther, a superb Biblical scholar, was also an excellent Christian theologian who easily dismantled the superficial Biblical and theological arguments in favor of the Papacy. Because of this rich display of Christian wisdom, his radical criticism cannot be explained in psychological terms as if he were driven by resentment only. His theological assessments set the tone for the wider Reformation movement.

CALVIN'S 'ANTIDOTES' TO THE PAPACY

The French Reformer John Calvin dealt with Roman Catholic representatives at various times and in different ways.[28] His major work, the *Institutes of the Christian Religion* (first edition: 1536) contains frequent interactions with Roman Catholic doctrines and practices. Here Calvin develops his argument that the Pope is the Antichrist (*Institutes* IV, 7, 25). The historical Pope that Calvin had in view was Paul III (1534–49), but his critique never focuses on his person but rather on the Papal institution. After underlining that the Antichrist sets his tyranny in opposition to the spiritual kingdom of Christ, Calvin writes that the Antichrist 'abolishes not the name of either Christ or the Church, but rather uses the name of Christ as a pretext, and lurks under the name of Church as under a mask' by robbing God of his honor. This is for him a clear picture of the Pope and therefore he concludes by saying that 'it is certain that the Roman Pontiff has impudently transferred to himself the most peculiar properties of God and Christ, there cannot be a doubt that he is the leader and standard-bearer of an impious and abominable kingdom'. Calvin is not speaking of a particular historical Pope, but of the Pope as representing the institution of the Papacy.

Protestant arguments against the Papacy do not concentrate on personalities and characters, but on its faulty biblical foundations and dangerous theological consequences.

Calvin's main critical analysis of the Papacy is found in two works in particular. In 1543 the theological faculty of the Sorbonne published twenty-five articles that candidates had to subscribe to as a kind of oath to remain faithful to the Catholic Church. The following year, Calvin wrote a refutation of this summary of Catholic doctrine in his *Articuli a facultate sacrae theologiae parisiensi* by quoting each article and providing a critical review, i.e. an 'antidote'.[29] Article XXIII treats the primacy of the See of Rome and rehearses Catholic proofs for it. In response, Calvin argues that while Scripture often speaks of Christ as the head of the Church, it never does so as far as the Pope is concerned.[30] The unity of the Church is based on one God, one faith and one baptism (Eph. 4:4), but there is no mention of the necessity of a pope in order for the Church to be the Church. Moreover, in listing the ministries and offices of the Church, Paul is silent about a present or future Papacy. Peter was Paul's co-worker, not his pope-like leader. The universal Bishop of the Church is Christ alone. To this Biblical argument for the headship of Christ, Calvin adds a historical reference to Patristic writings that support the same New Testament view. Even Cyprian of Carthage, often considered a Church Father who favored an early form of a Papacy, calls the bishop of Rome a 'brother, fellow-Christian, and colleague in the episcopate', thus showing that he did not have in view the kind of primacy that was later attributed to the Pope. These kinds of Biblical and patristic arguments against the Papacy can be found in another giant of the Protestant Reformation of the sixteenth century, namely Peter Martyr Vermigli (1499–1562), especially in his 1542 *Trattato della vera chiesa e della necessità di viver in essa* (Treatise of the true church and the necessity to live in her).[31] They appear to be standard controversial treatments of the magisterial Reformation.

Returning to Calvin, another of his works that deals with the Papacy was written in 1549. When Charles V tried to find a compromise solution to the Augsburg Interim, Bucer and Bullinger urged Calvin to respond. He wrote the treatise *Vera Christianae pacificationis et Ecclesiae reformandae ratio* in which he described the doctrines that should be upheld, including justification by faith. In expounding the doctrine of the Church, Calvin devotes a section to the Papacy. Here he criticizes the standard Roman Catholic reading of John 21, a New Testament text considered to be one of the Biblical foundations of the Papal office. In commenting on the passage, Calvin notes that the threefold command to Peter to shepherd the sheep is to be related to Peter's threefold denial of Jesus. This office is not exclusive, given that Peter exhorts his fellow-elders to do the same (1 Peter 5:2). Furthermore, according to Calvin, the Papacy is totally invalid because in the New Testament there is no injunction given to Peter to find successors in a juridical sense. To keep the unity of the Church, Christ is all we need. Calvin then comments on the choice of Rome as the chosen See for the Pope. Why Rome? Calvin asks. In writing to the Romans, Paul mentions many individual names, but Peter is not on the list. And even if Peter would later go to Rome, why was the city selected as the special and central place for future Popes? Why not Jerusalem? Or Antioch? Calvin, however, does not address the political and historical importance of Rome as reasons for locating the Papacy there.

Finally, Calvin once again accuses the Pope of being the Antichrist because of his 'tyranny', 'destruction of the truth', 'corruption of the worship of God', 'breaking of His ordinances', and the 'dispersion of the order of His Church'. Here we see many similarities with Luther, except that with Calvin the apocalyptic tone is not as strong and is less evident than that of the German reformer. Rather than passionate eschatological concerns, Calvin relies on lucid theological and Biblical arguments in his effort to identify the Pope as the Antichrist.

TURRETIN'S DISPUTATION ON THE ANTICHRIST

The identification of the Antichrist with the Pope is not solely a Protestant fixation of the first generation of Reformers. It became the standard Protestant view even after the sixteenth century and is found in the works of individual theologians and in the Protestant confessions of faith that consolidated the doctrinal heritage of the Reformation. *The Westminster Confession of Faith* (1647), for example, reflects the common consensus of Reformed churches when it states that 'There is no other head of the Church but the Lord Jesus Christ. Nor can the pope of Rome, in any sense, be head thereof, but is that

Antichrist, the man of sin, and son of perdition, that exalteth himself, in the church, against Christ and all that is called God' (art. XXV. 6).[32]

Francis Turretin (1623–87) is perhaps the greatest Reformed theologian of the seventeenth century. His major work, the *Institutes of Elenctic Theology*, has been one of the most influential theological textbooks of the continental Reformed tradition. In his section on the Church, Turretin extensively deals with the Papacy, as he always engages in 'apologetic' theology. His more comprehensive treatment of the Pope as the Antichrist, however, is his *7th Disputation on the Antichrist* that, in turn, is part of a larger work entitled *Concerning our Necessary Secession from the Church of Rome and the Impossibility of Cooperation with Her* (1661).[33] Here we find perhaps the most detailed and systematic Protestant argument for the identification of the Pope as the Antichrist. Turretin endeavors to exegete Scripture and evaluate the facts of church history for the purpose of saving the Church of Christ from committing spiritual fornication.[34]

After noting that it is the common opinion of Protestants that the Pope is the Antichrist, Turretin explains that Scripture reveals the place of the Antichrist (the temple), his time (from apostolic times onward), and his person (an apostate from the faith, a performer of spurious miracles, one who opposes Christ, a self-exalting figure, a man of sin, an idolater). Turretin goes as far as analyzing the name and number of the Beast of Revelation 13:17–18. Gathering these elements together, he does not find these marks among the Jews or Turks (Muslims), nor among the Greek Orthodox. In his view, they only fit the chief authority of the Roman Church.

Turretin is convinced that the Antichrist is not a single person but must refer to an office or succession of persons in office that began operating in apostolic times. To the Roman Catholic objection that Popes have never denied Christ, Turretin replies that the Antichrist will not openly deny Christ as a professed enemy but as a professed friend of Christ who praises Him with their words, yet fights Him with his actions. He sees this attitude in Popes who arrogate to themselves the three offices of Christ (Priest, Prophet and King), but bury the Gospel under their own traditions and undermine His work of redemption by their masses, purgatory, indulgences, and false worship.

These views are far from 'ecumenically correct' and may be perceived as totally off the mark. Yet, whatever one makes of them, it is important to appreciate that they do not stem from slandering invectives or bandying insults. Theologians like Turretin built a highly sophisticated Biblical and theological argument and were not driven by resentment alone. One should also bear in mind that the Catholic counter-apologetic of the time used similar language in attacking the tenets of the Reformation.

5

ABSOLUTE RULER OR EMBRACING FATHER?

THE PAPACY FROM THE COUNTER-REFORMATION TO THE ECUMENICAL MOVEMENT

The Protestant Reformation was an opportunity for the Papal institution to rethink its imperial structure and monarchical power. Prior to the Reformation, there had been many voices suggesting a re-balancing of the relationship between the Councils and Popes, the need for spiritual renewal of the exercise of Church authority, the emphasis on personal integrity in the Papal lifestyle, and a call to re-focus on the spiritual tasks of the Church over against its prevailing secular interests. Above all the

Reformation was meant to be an opportunity to address the theological framework of the Papacy by leading it towards a more biblically defined outlook.

A couple of centuries later, the affirmation of modernity in science, philosophy, politics and religious ideology further challenged the Papacy to revise its absolute stance. The initial responses to the Reformation and the Enlightenment were extremely negative, if not harsh. At the end of the ninteenth century, many thought that the Papacy was about to capitulate to the pressures of the modern world. However, the Papacy is a living institution and the twentieth century has witnessed its impressive resurgence. Present-day Popes are global celebrities who have embraced much of what their predecessors had severely criticized, or totally rejected, while maintaining the core elements of the historically stratified self-understanding of the Papacy.

COUNTER-REFORMATION POPES

As the Reformation began to sweep across Europe, Popes were unprepared to face the challenge in a constructive way. Although Julius II (1503–13) convoked the Fifth Lateran Council (1511–17) to debate various reforms, their reaction was marked by an attempt to suppress the Reformation using the disciplinary tools at their disposal—excommunication and repression. Although it was Leo X that excommunicated Luther in 1521, Paul IV (1555–9) was the first Pope to issue the Index of Prohibited Books (*Index Librorum Prohibitorum*), which contained mostly Protestant authors. He forbade that they be read, or possessed. Even translations of the Bible were among the forbidden books. The vehement attack against the translations allowed the historian Gigliola Fragnito to speak of 'the Bible on a stake' to describe what happened in countries dominated by the Catholic Church. The ban lasted for centuries.[35]

Even though the Inquisition (i.e. a special religious tribunal) had been active since the twelfth century to fight heresies, it was Paul III that in 1542 established the Congregation of the Holy Office of the Inquisition as a permanent authority staffed with Cardinals and other officials.[36] By improving its efficacy, Pius V (1566–72) used it to try to eradicate Protestant influences in majority Roman Catholic territories. He even built a new palace for the Inquisition next to St. Peter's basilica. The victims of the Inquisition were not only Protestants, but also all those who were perceived as threats to the stability of the Papal system, such as free thinkers like Giordano Bruno (burned at the stake in 1600), and scientists like Galileo Galilei (who had to recant his writings in 1633 after being condemned).

As the Protestant challenge to Roman Catholicism progressed successfully into the sixteenth century, calls for a general council to address the question of Church reform and to develop strategies to meet the Protestant threat grew louder, especially from Emperor Charles V (1519–56). Under duress, Pope Paul III (1534–49) opened the first session of the Council of Trent in 1545. Paul recognized the need for reform but resented imperial pressure to call for a council that might rival papal authority within the Church. In the Bull of Indiction in 1542 he stated that the purpose of the Council would be 'to maintain the Christian religion in its integrity, and to confirm within us the hope of heavenly things; the unity of the Christian name was rent and well-nigh torn asunder by schisms, dissensions, heresies'.

The Council of Trent met sporadically over the next three decades in three sessions (1545–7; 1551–2; 1562–3) broken up by political infighting, papal deaths, and outbreaks of plague. Although disjointed, the council nevertheless resulted in a spectacular resurgence of Roman Catholicism and, with the simultaneous development of the Jesuit order, capped a period of retrenchment and renewal known as the Catholic Counter-Reformation.[37] At Trent, Roman Catholic leaders rejected all attempts to compromise with Protestantism and retained the basic positions of the Roman Church, including the Latin Mass, the veneration of saints, the cult of the Virgin Mary, and the notion that salvation required both faith and good works. They defended Roman Catholic theology and emphasized reforms, ordering an end to abuses of power and corruption within the clergy and established seminaries to educate priests. Finally, Trent came out strongly in support of papal power, strengthening the authority of the papacy. In its *Decree on Reformation* in Session XV (1563), the Council reinforced it in these terms: 'the holy Synod declares, that all and singular the things which, under whatsoever clauses and words, have been ordained in this sacred Council, in the matter of

The Council of Trent was the official response of the Roman Catholic Church to the sixteenth century Protestant Reformation. The issues of the Reformation (grace alone, faith alone, Christ alone) were rejected as they were affirmed by the Reformers (mainly Luther) and recast in a sacramental framework that highlighted the contribution of human works and the mediating agency of the church. Trent declared the Reformation incompatible with what then became the official doctrine of the Church of Rome. It solidified the theology of the sacraments, hitting those who held Protestant beliefs with a series of 'anathema'. Trent clarified the Roman position (through decrees and canons) and launched a series of changes that would impact the life of the Church.

The Council was not an isolated event. A staunch polemical attitude marked the post-Trent phase of the Church, first against Protestantism, and then against modernity. If Trent was the Roman response to the Reformation, the Marian dogmas (immaculate conception of Mary, 1854; bodily assumption of Mary, 1950, and papal infallibility, 1870) were responses to the ideological challenges of Modernity. Five centuries on, the Roman Church has adopted a different pastoral and ecclesial 'style' to Trent, but it has not substantially changed it, nor denied it. At no point does Vatican II move away from the dogmatic teaching of Trent, but keeps it in the background and within the Roman Catholic framework. The 'Tridentine paradigm' was put in historical perspective, but not forsaken. Vatican II metabolized Trent, but did not abandon it.

With the 1999 'Joint Declaration on the Doctrine of Justification' between the Roman Catholic Church and the World Lutheran Federation, Trent's language and emphases were updated, but reiterated in substance. The two positions were juxtaposed and held compatible, thus working with a 'both-and' scheme that is quintessentially the Roman Catholic way of developing its doctrinal system. Tridentine 'anathemas' were lifted for those who reinterpreted ecumenically the Reformation doctrines, but the theological core of contemporary Roman Catholicism is still steeped in its Tridentine content: the institutional church mediates the grace of God through its sacramental system. Grace alone was and is rejected; nothing has changed in important areas like indulgences, Purgatory, the sacramental prerogatives of the Church, and the cult of the saints.

reformation of morals, and ecclesiastical discipline, as well under the Sovereign Pontiffs, Paul III, and Julius III, of happy memory, as under the most blessed Pius IV, have been so decreed, as that the authority of the Apostolic See both is, and is understood to be, untouched thereby' (chapter XXIII).

In short, the Catholic Reformation, and especially the Council of Trent, stopped the momentum of the Protestant Reformation and set the stage for an escalation of religious warfare throughout Europe, for example, the Thirty Years' War (1618–48). In terms of religious affiliation, the Roman Catholic church began to regain large parts of the continent, and by 1650 at least half of all Protestants had reconverted. The Tridentine zeal also impacted foreign missionary activities. Pope Gregory XV founded the Congregation of Propaganda Fide in 1622, an organization whose task was to arrange missionary work on behalf of the various religious institutions in non-Catholic lands. In 1627, Urban VIII established a training college for missionaries. The 'victory' over the Protestant heresy was also celebrated with the exuberant and excessive style of the baroque. The Popes wanted the arts to communicate religious themes stemming from the Counter-Reformation with direct and emotional involvement. The city of Rome was significantly shaped by the baroque style by artists such as Gian Lorenzo Bernini (1598–1680) and Francesco Borromini (1599–1667). If St. Peter's basilica epitomizes the grandeur of the imperial and victorious church, with all its splendor and power, Bernini's colonnade in front of the basilica (1656–67) wonderfully portrays the two arms of the Church, stretched out and ready to embrace the world. After the challenge of the Reformation, the Papacy successfully emerged from it and not only confirmed its previous outlook, but became even stronger and more reinforced in its universal mission.

EX-CATHEDRA INFALLIBILITY

In the seventeenth century the Papacy had to face two staunch adversaries that were able to challenge its survival.[38] On the political level, there was the absolutism of princes and European states that claimed power over the Church, thus questioning the difficult balance between powers that had been reached in previous centuries. The political struggle reached its peak with the French Revolution first and then with Napoleon. Breaking the long established tradition by which Popes would crown kings, Napoleon crowned himself and claimed the right to appoint bishops. It was only after Napoleon's defeat and the Congress of Vienna (1814–15) that the Papacy recovered its position among the European powers and attempted to reverse the course of history. The Popes, however, had been irreversibly perceived as part of the *Ancien Régime* (Old regime) which the modern world would soon overcome on many fronts.

On the philosophical front, the spread of the Enlightenment clashed with the traditional worldview of the Papacy. The insistence on the prominence of 'reason' over the 'superstition' of religions, the growing importance of evolutionary theory over more static accounts of reality, and the diffusion of socialist ideas against the mere protection of the *status quo* caused Popes to react strongly in order to safeguard their share in the established system of power. In the Encyclical *Mirari Vos* (1832) Gregory XVI condemned all systems of thought that were contrary to the faith, such as rationalism and indifferentism. He went as far as condemning all modern liberties, such as free circulation of books, any form of dissent, and separation of church and state. According to Gregory XVI, even freedom of conscience was a 'pestilence' to be avoided like poison. In the nineteenth century, Popes developed a harsh, critical stance towards what they perceived to be mortal dangers for religion, stability, and the established order of things. This negative attitude reached a climax in 1864 when Pius IX issued the *Symbol of Errors*, a list of statements that were condemned by the Pope. Apart from banning modern philosophical ideas, religious freedom and the activities of Bible Societies, the *Symbol* included the following

After receiving an invitation from Pius IX to attend the First Vatican Council, Charles Hodge of Princeton Theological Seminary responded on behalf of two General Assemblies of the Presbyterian Church in the USA. In declining the invitation, and after explaining that Protestants are not heretics or schismatics, Hodge wrote: 'Much less can we recognize the Bishop of Rome as the vicar of Christ on earth, clothed with the authority over the Church and the world which was exercised by our Lord while here in the flesh. It is plain that no one can be the vicar of Christ who has not the attributes of Christ. To recognize the Bishop of Rome as Christ's vicar is therefore virtually to recognize him as divine.'

statement that the Pope rejected: 'The Roman Pontiff can, and ought to, reconcile himself, and come to terms with, progress, liberalism and modern civilization' (80).

The Pope thought of himself as separate from the modern world. The clash could not have been more strident. A similar sweeping condemnation was also issued against Roman Catholic intellectuals who sympathized with aspects of modern ideas. Their movement was therefore derogatorily called 'Modernism'. According to Pius X, modernism was 'the synthesis of all heresies' (*Pascendi Dominici Gregis*, 1907). In the midst of this rising turmoil, Pius IX (1846–78) promulgated the dogma of the Immaculate conception of Mary (1954), a belief that Mary, as the future mother of the sinless Son of God, was preserved from original sin at conception. As the Pope was denouncing the errors of modernity, he was at the same time defining an accepted way for the faithful. The expanded role of Mariology was just one response to the modern challenges the Church was facing.

This heavy atmosphere of an aggressive cultural siege was also the background to the First Vatican Council (1869–70). The felt danger of being assaulted by the modern world pushed Pius IX to insist that the Council clearly specify the juridical primacy of the Pope as far as the leadership of the Church is concerned and proclaim the infallibility of his teaching under certain conditions (Dogmatic Constitution *Pastor Aeternus*). Concerning the contours of the Papal office, here is what Vatican I declared:

If anyone, then, shall say that the Roman Pontiff has the office merely of inspection or direction, and not the full and supreme power of jurisdiction over the Universal Church, not only in things which belong to faith and morals, but also in those which relate to the discipline and government of the Church spread throughout the world; or assert that he possesses merely the principal part, and not all the fullness of this supreme power; or that this power which he enjoys is not ordinary and immediate, both over each and all the Churches and over each and all the Pastors and the faithful; let him be anathema'. (III)

As to Papal infallibility, *Pastor Aeternus* defines it like this:

We teach and define that it is a divinely-revealed dogma: that the Roman Pontiff, when he speaks *ex Cathedra*, that is, when in discharge of the office of Pastor and Teacher of all Christians, by virtue of his supreme Apostolic authority, he defines a doctrine regarding faith or morals to be held by the Universal Church, by the divine assistance promised to him in blessed Peter, is possessed of that infallibility with which the divine Redeemer willed that His Church should be endowed for defining doctrine regarding faith or morals: and that therefore such definitions of the Roman Pontiff are irreformable of themselves, and not from the consent of the Church. But if anyone—God forbid—should presume to contradict this Our definition; let him be anathema' (IV).[39]

The First Vatican Council provided the most comprehensive and authoritative doctrinal statement on the Papacy in the modern era. Instead of taking into account the Biblical critique legitimately offered by the Protestant Reformation, and instead of listening to certain trends of modern thought that advocate freedom of conscience and freedom of religion, Vatican I further solidified the nature of the Papal office as a quasi-omnipotent and infallible figure. The Roman Catholic Church invested its highest doctrinal authority, the promulgation of a dogma, a binding, irreversible, unchangeable truth, to cement the institution of the Papacy and further its absolute nature. The only Biblical argument given to support this dogma is the citation of Luke 22:32 (Jesus says to Peter: 'I prayed for you, so that your faith will not falter'). Yet, this citation does not support any of *Pastor Aeternus*'s definition in that Jesus in no way warrants Peter's future infallibility and absolute power, far less the infallibility and powers of future Popes. As it is the case with much of the doctrine of the Papacy, this last doctrinal formulation, while further strengthening the dogma, is also founded on extra-Biblical arguments.

The tragic irony of this Council was that its proceedings had to be abruptly stopped because the Italian army entered the city of Rome, and proclaimed it the capital of the newly reunited nation. The Vatican State lost nearly all its territories and the Pope was confined within the Vatican walls as if he were a prisoner. Pius IX, the first infallible Pope, was also the last Pope who reigned like a king. It was as if the modern world, which the nineteenth-century Popes had severely condemned, took revenge and almost entirely swept the Papal claims away. The year

1870 marked the highest doctrinal claims of the Papacy and perhaps the lowest moment of its history.

'AGGIORNAMENTO' (UPDATING) OF THE PAPACY

The nineteenth century seemed to end in a *cul-de-sac* for the Papacy. If there were a movie on the topic, an appropriate title would be 'The Pope Against the World'. The story, however, did not end here. Soon after the condemnations of modernity and the dogmatic expressions of Papal infallibility, there were Popes that showed more humanitarian concerns for the difficult conditions of the working class and a more open attitude towards listening to the cries of the modern world. In 1891, for instance, Leo XIII (1878–1903) published the encyclical *Rerum Novarum* in which he adressed social justice issues, focusing on the rights and duties of capital and labor. For the first time, a Pope would at least recognize the problem. This document became the springboard of the Social Doctrine of the Church that was developed by later Popes and is now a stabilized part of the Roman Catholic magisterium.[40] Centered around ideas like personhood, subsidiarity, solidarity, and community, the Social Doctrine of the Church is one of the pillars of the present-day witness of the Roman Catholic Church in the world. Going back to Leo XIII, scholars are beginning to see interesting parallels between the social awareness of this Pope and that of his contemporary, the Dutch reformed theologian and statesman Abraham Kuyper.[41]

After centuries of Catholic embarrassment regarding the Bible, Leo XIII was also active in encouraging the study of Scripture, as is evidenced by his encyclical *Providentissimus Deus* (1893). Because of his mild openness to reform, some scholars see in his reign the beginnings of the 'Evangelical Catholicism' that was later expounded by the Second Vatican Council (1962–5), found its champion in John Paul II (1978–2005), and was again reinforced by Benedict XVI (2005–13).[42] This account of 'Evangelical Catholicism' is the combination of Roman Catholic doctrine and Evangelical zeal. One ought to bear in mind that Leo XIII was also a strong advocate of Marian devotion and other Catholic practices that are difficult to square with an 'Evangelical' outlook. With his encyclical *Aeterni Patris* (1879) Pope Leo elevated 'the sacred doctrine of St. Thomas Aquinas' to be the standard theological system of the Catholic Church.

These signs of change were also counter-balanced by more conservative and even reactionary moves of other Popes who reaffirmed the opposition of the Church to the modern world (Pius X) and modern theology (Pius XII). The tragedy of the two world wars in the twentieth century saw the Popes either launch appeals for peace (Benedict XV, 1914–22) or assume a low-profile in the conflict in order to safeguard the interests of the Church (Pius XII, 1939–58). In 1950, during a time of turmoil, Pius XII explicitly invoked Papal infallibility with the dogma of the Assumption of Mary. This dogma states that Mary, 'having completed the course of her earthly life, was assumed body and soul into heavenly glory'

(*Munificentissimus Deus*, 44). This is the last dogma that the Roman Catholic Church has issued in its long history.

The more 'catholic' trajectory of present-day Popes found a memorable interpreter in John XXIII (1958–63). He called the church to a time of 'aggiornamento', that is updating the posture of the Church in relationship to the world without changing the traditional doctrine. A theologically conservative Pope, he came to be known as 'Good Pope John' for his fatherly and warm attitude. Gentle in spirit, meek in manners, approachable by the people, Roncalli was the first modern Pope to be seen not as a king, but as a pastor. His language was simple and his human frame was humble. Unsurprisingly, his main achievement (Vatican II) was meant to be a 'pastoral' council. John XXIII did not want a rigidly 'doctrinal' church that would judge the mistakes of the world, but a loving 'mother' who would offer protection and understanding for all. He convened the Second Vatican Council (1962–5) to induce the Church to re-think its over-critical approach inherited by Vatican I and to embrace a more 'catholic', universal, outlook. He wanted the Church to be the 'mother' of the world, not its 'enemy'. If Vatican I had pushed the Roman Church to clash with modernity, Vatican II tried to encourage new ways of engaging with the challenges and the opportunities of the twentieth century world. The radical opposition towards Biblical criticism, scientific evolution, religious freedom, socialist ideas, democracy, and other modern practices was changed into a welcoming, discerning and more open approach towards the heart of the modern mind

Was Vatican II progressive or traditionalist? Did it intend to reform the Church or to reinforce it? Was it doctrinally focused or more pastorally oriented? Was it primarily an 'event' or did it initiate a 'movement'?

There are two main schools of thought. One interpretative school sees Vatican II as breaking with the traditional RC outlook and bringing a progressive trend to the Church. This has been the direction of theologians like Hans Küng and historians like Giuseppe Alberigo. According to this interpretation, while Vatican II introduced significant 'change', Paul VI, John Paul II and Benedict XVI silenced its potential in areas like ecclesiology, liturgy, and morality, imposing a rigid reading that squares with the traditional self-understanding of the Roman Church. Traditionalists like Msgr. Lefebvre shared this view. He charged Vatican II with betraying RC identity, having marred it with mortal doses of Protestant and secular poison. The same interpretation of Vatican II's discontinuity with the past therefore produced opposing reactions.

The mainstream interpretative school, however, insists that Vatican II stands in continuity with Vatican I (1870–71), completing what was left unfinished. No 'real' change occurred, only a dynamic re-statement of the well established RC heritage. At Vatican II the RC Church approached the modern world in more 'pastoral' terms, without modifying its framework. According to this linear reading, Vatican II at most brought an 'aggiornamento' (updating) to the language and the concerns of the Church, while maintaining her fundamental stance.

Recently, this debate has been revived. In a 2005 speech Benedict XVI said the Council needs to be read according to a 'hermeneutics of reform-in-continuity'. In a restricted sense it was a 'reforming' Council, yet Vatican II simply reiterated the RC dogmatic system without altering it. In this sense, the Council is in continuity with Trent and Vatican I. The RC understanding of historical development entails 'reform-in-continuity', 'aggiornamento' without renouncing, addition without subtraction, expansion without purification. Unless one grasps this 'both-and' approach, one will fall prey to fragmented and insufficient accounts of Roman Catholicism. 'Reform-in-continuity' is its genius.

and soul. Previously defined as 'heretics', Protestants were instead referred to as 'separated brethren'. Non-Christian religions were seen as friendly partners in the search for truth. The Church that had severely criticized the Ecumenical Movement of the beginning of the XX century became one of its strongest supporters, although having its own ecumenical agenda.

After Vatican II, Paul VI (1963–78) began the tradition of the Traveling Popes, visiting countries never before visited by a Pope. The Pope ceased to be a static figure, always residing in Rome and quintessentially associated with the life of the Eternal city. He became a 'universal' pastor that would travel extensively to reach the global world. Some of the most unpalatable features of the 'imperial' heritage of the Papacy (i.e. dressing codes, the display of symbols of power) were no longer used, yet never formally abrogated.

The 'catholic' trend of the Papacy was further implemented by John Paul II (1978) who took center stage and captured the world's attention. This 'show-Pope' massively used the modern media (e.g. above all television), dramatically intensified the global character of the Papacy, and attuned this old and traditional institution with the concerns of the poor of the world. With John Paul II the Papacy ceased to be merely an Italian and Western institution, becoming instead a significant player in world history. It is now appropriate to dedicate a more thorough attention to the last three Popes: John Paul II, Benedict XVI, and Francis.

6

PORTRAITS OF PRESENT-DAY POPES

JOHN PAUL II, BENEDICT XVI, FRANCIS

The role of the Pope has been interpreted differently throughout history. There have been different kinds of Pope. For most people, however, the only Popes they remember are the last three: John Paul II, Benedict XVI, and Francis. Although Pius XII in 1931 was the first Pope to use the radio to broadcast his message, John Paul II was the first televised Pope, becoming the first 'global' and 'celebrity' Pope who shaped the Papacy and the perception of the Papacy much more powerfully than his predecessors. Benedict XVI was the intellectual Pope who tried to call the West back to its Catholic roots. Francis is the reigning Pope who comes from 'the end of the world' and who is trying to reinvigorate this old institution while maintaining its post-Vatican II doctrinal balance. Let us look at their individual portraits in order to critically evaluate their specific contribution.

THE UNSETTLED LEGACY OF JOHN PAUL II

Karol Wojtyła (1920–2005), since 1978 better known as Pope John Paul II, was one of the most influential men of the twentieth century. A quick look at the titles of biographies about him shows the magnitude of the man: 'The man of the end of the millennium' (L. Accattoli), 'Witness to hope' (G. Weigel), 'The man of the century' (J. Kwitny), 'Pilgrim of the absolute' (G. Reale), 'The defeater of communism' (A. Santini). As is always the case with human biographies, celebrative voices abound as well as critical readings. Other titles point to the controversial aspects of his life: 'Victory and decline' (C. Cardia), 'The Pope in Winter: The Dark Face of John Paul II's Papacy' (J. Cornwell), 'The Wojtyła enigma' (J. Arias), 'The last Pope king' (L. Sandri).

His life was at the centre of the major affairs of the twentieth century: the tragedy of Nazism and the trauma of the Second World War, the apex and fall of Communism, the Second Vatican Council and its debated implementation, the apparent triumph of Western democracy and the oppressive costs of globalization for the Majority world, the fracture of ideologies and the rise of secular hedonism. Wojtyła played a significant role in all these major events. Supporters have acclaimed his achievements in terms of navigating, surviving and overcoming the dangerous streams of our post-something world. Critics have pointed out the double-faced, contradictory trajectory of his life and his backward looking Roman Catholic outlook.

How do we assess John Paul II's legacy? Because of the stature of the man, the question is overwhelming in every respect. Amongst the vast number of books available, one guide worth noting is Tim Perry's edited book, *The Legacy of John Paul II: An Evangelical Assessment*[43]—one of the few attempts to provide an evaluation from a Conservative Protestant point of view. The book bears witness to the fact that it was under John Paul II that Evangelical attitudes toward Roman Catholicism began to change and become friendly, if not even cooperative. This was the Pope who called his Church to be engaged in mission, encouraged the pro-life front, welcomed some Evangelical concerns in relation to Bible literacy and liturgical variety, and seemed to be closer to the Majority world than his predecessors. Perry also shows that even some Reformed thinkers today speak of the Pope as 'Holy Father'[44]—something that is not biblically natural. Moreover, in evaluating the overall theology of his fourteen encyclicals, some conservative Protestant theologians can say that it is 'Bible-based, humanity-focused, Christ-centered and mission-attuned[45]—something that sounds like a full endorsement.

Certainly there has been a significant shift of attitude and John Paul II has made an impression on many Evangelicals. The book edited by Perry contains positive comments on each encyclical signed by Wojtyła and the tone is close to admiration, despite some minor criticism. Much of it is a fair summary of what the Pope wrote, yet it is selective in many ways. For instance, there is no mention that each encyclical ends with an invocation to Mary, which does not represent a Christocentric and biblical pattern. Moreover, there is little recognition that, besides the Bible, papal encyclicals quote even more extensively from sources of the tradition of the Church. The Bible is only *one* source amongst many, and apparently not the decisive one. On specific contents,

On April 30, 2011 John Paul II was beatified and on April 27, 2014, he was canonized. During the course of his beatification, the Saturday night Marian prayer vigil was an attempt to honor the Marianism of the former Pope and to commend it to the faithful. The open air vigil commenced with a procession behind the Maria Salus Populi Romani ('Mary the salvation of the Roman people'), a Byzantine Marian icon deemed to be the protector of the Romans, followed by her enthronement at Circus Maximum. The elevation of the icon is a symbol of Mary being the object of public hyper-veneration (the unique tribute of honor that the RC Church pays to her). The crowd then joined in singing the hymn Totus Tuus ('Wholly yours'), echoing John Paul II's motto that indicated his total commitment to Mary. A Marian rosary followed in a satellite link with five Marian sanctuaries: Krakow (Poland), Bugando (Tanzania), Harissa (Lebanon), Guadalupe (Mexico). and Fatima (Portugal). John Paul II visited all these places during his long pontificate and video excerpts of his speeches on Mary were shown on large screens. During the night the crowd was encouraged to join in prayers to Mary. The beatification ceremonies were a great boost to Marian spirituality.

Faith and Ratio (*Faith and Reason*, 1998) combines Aristotelian reason and Thomistic faith, leaving out many Biblical strands. *Ecclesia de Eucharistia* (*The Church from the Eucharist*, 2003) reinforces the traditional RC doctrine of the sacrificial nature of the Eucharist, its re-enactment of Jesus' death and the practice of adoration of the host. *Ut Unum Sint* (*That They Be One*, 1995) claims that the Pope is willing to change the forms of his universal ministry, but not the substance of his Petrine office, which supplements the headship of Christ on the church. *Redemptoris Mater* (*The Mother of the Redeemer*, 1987) is a Marian-centered re-telling of salvation history, something the Bible does not encourage. The list could go on and on, yet one point must be further elaborated.

Marian devotion was a feature of John Paul II's life. He believed the so-called secrets of Fatima, in which Mary played a decisive role, diverting the bullet when terrorist Ali Ağca shot the Pope in 1981. Apparently, the Pope believed in Marian providence, considering Mary a major player in world affairs, earthly and cosmic, material and spiritual. For this reason, along with the human family and a new century, he dedicated planet earth to her at the beginning of the new millennium, pleading for constant protection and guidance. Moreover, his personal motto was *totus tuus*, totally yours—'yours' referring to Mary.

BENEDICT XVI'S ROMAN CATHOLIC ORTHODOXY

Assessing a pontificate is no easy task. Assessing Benedict's pontificate (2005–13) is even more difficult.

The caliber of Ratzinger as a theologian, the muddy state of present-day Vatican affairs, and the complexity of global religious and moral trends are all factors that call for careful consideration, although his pontificate will perhaps be remembered more for the surprising way it ended than for what it achieved. Our task here will be modest. It will take as parameters the main bullet points that characterized Evangelical perceptions of Benedict's pontificate.[46] It will be an exercise to see to what extent they match reality.

A recurring comment is that Benedict XVI has been an 'orthodox' pope. In this case, orthodox means maintaining Nicene Christianity, the Trinitarian and Christological confession of faith of the early church. In itself, being 'orthodox' is not a distinct feature of any single Pope because it is part of his service. The pope, or any pope, is to be 'orthodox'. Bonifacius VIII, the pope that introduced the papal tiara in 1300 (indicative of the temporal power), was 'orthodox'. Pope Leo X, the one who excommunicated Martin Luther in 1521, was 'orthodox'. The best and the worst Popes were 'orthodox'. Indeed, all 266 Popes since Peter (taking for granted that Peter was the first Pope) have been 'orthodox'. The business of the Pope is to be 'orthodox' in this Nicene sense.

It may be true that Benedict put a special emphasis on orthodoxy, but he interpreted his orthodoxy in a Roman Catholic way, like all previous Popes. He prayed daily to Mary, granted indulgences, canonized new saints, and maintained the church-state profile of the Vatican. Contrary to what C.S. Lewis believed, there

In the 2010 Post-Synodical Apostolic Exhortation, *Verbum Domini* (The Word of the Lord), Benedict XVI wrote that the Word of God 'precedes and exceeds sacred Scripture, nonetheless Scripture, as inspired by God, contains the divine word' (17). *Verbum Domini* claims that the Bible is the Word of God in the sense that it contains the Word. There is the Bible and there is also a further word beyond the Bible that makes the Bible insufficient on its own. What is at stake here is not the divine inspiration of the Bible (which *Verbum Domini* firmly affirms), but the sufficiency and finality of the Bible. For Pope Ratzinger, the Bible is the Word of God in some sense, but the Word of God is bigger than the Bible. The latter contains the former.

Liberal theology has developed its own theology of the Word whereby the relationship between the Word and the Bible is thought of in dialectical and existential ways. In other words, for some versions of liberal theology, the Bible is a (fallible) testimony to the Word and it becomes the Word of God, if ever, when the Spirit speaks through it. The RC version of the Word-Bible relationship is articulated in a different way. The premise is the same (the Bible contains the Word), but the outworking of the Word comes through the tradition of the RC Church. The gap between the Word and the Bible is not existential but ecclesial. The Church is the cradle of the Word, both in its past and written form (the Bible) and in its on-going utterances (Tradition). In this respect, Benedict XVI writes: 'The Church lives in the certainty that her Lord, who spoke in the past, continues today to communicate his word in her living Tradition and in sacred Scripture. Indeed, the word of God given to us in sacred Scripture as an inspired testimony to revelation, together with the Church's living Tradition, it constitutes the supreme rule of faith' (18). The Bible is upheld, but it is always accompanied and surmounted by the wider, deeper, living tradition of the Church which is the present-day form of the Word. Amongst other things, this means that the Bible is insufficient in itself to give access to the Word and is not the final norm for faith and practice. The Bible needs to be supplemented by the Catechism of the Catholic Church which is 'a significant expression of the living Tradition of the Church and a sure norm for teaching the faith' (74) is no 'mere orthodoxy' out there. Nicene Christianity is always colored by subsequent developments in Christian doctrine and practice. It never stands in isolation nor exists in an abstract way. Benedict's pontificate has been a peak of Roman Catholic orthodoxy.

It is true that in his catechetical efforts, Benedict dealt with the Bible much more than his immediate predecessors. His speeches have largely been Biblical meditations and his recent writings on Jesus defended the historicity of the Gospel accounts. Much of his reading of Scripture, however, was driven by post-biblical presuppositions that come out of ecclesiastical tradition rather than Scripture. The heavily sacramental interpretations of Gospel stories and the over-arching interpretive grid that sees the relationship between Biblical teaching and Roman Catholic practices in terms of linear continuity, are only two examples of 'how' Biblical Benedict's magisterium has been. During his pontificate, the point that distinguished Roman Catholicism from the Protestant tradition was no longer whether or not the Bible is accessible to the people, but 'how' it is to be read and lived out.

There is still another aspect to bear in mind. The Pope's most famous (and criticized) speech, the 2006 Regensburg lecture, was not about Islam, but revolved around the need to keep the Hellenized combination of 'faith and reason' that Thomas Aquinas refined and to which the Roman Catholic Church adheres. In denouncing the threats to the 'classic' synthesis, Benedict indicated the 'sola Scriptura' of the Reformation as a major breach that eventually caused theological liberalism and present-day relativism. It is interesting that a 'Biblical' Pope would have such a low view of the Reformation's formal principle that brought the Bible back to the center of Church life.

Benedict has courageously stood for basic Judeo-Christian convictions about life, the family, and the welfare of society characterized by freedom and solidarity, even in the midst of criticism from secular intellectual circles. Like his predecessor, John Paul II, Benedict was commended by Muslim and other religious leaders for his tenacious defense of traditional morality in the global world. His Church, however, did not perform well in terms of public transparency and integrity concerning sexual abuse scandals, opaque financial manoeuvres, and appalling intrigues within the Vatican. During Benedict's reign the distinction between the standards of the official Church and those of the world were thin. He is not to blame for all this, yet this poor 'public' performance sheds light on the overall picture. This is perhaps one of the reasons why Benedict came to the almost unprecedented conclusion to resign from the papal office.

The Pope spoke of Christians as a 'minority' and encouraged the Church to re-think its identity accordingly. The fact that he did not take any action to move his Church beyond the privileged status it has in many countries where Roman Catholics are a majority puts his record as a 'public truth' teller in perspective. Would it not be a 'public truth' argument to say that the Church wants to be the church only, and not a religious agency with a built in state with its own politics, bank, and army, like any other state?

The New Evangelization was the idea of John Paul II, but Benedict XVI started implementing it by creating a dedicated Vatican office and making it the central theme of the 2012 Synod of Bishops. Pope Ratzinger came to terms with the idea that the West is largely post-Christian and in need of being evangelized again by a reinvigorated Church.

The future will tell what the New Evangelization will bring about in terms of spiritual renewal. Yet, so far there has been little self-criticism on the Church's part as to why the West became more secularized. Does the Church have any responsibility for the secular 'schism' that has taken place? No clear answer has come from Pope Ratzinger who has instead blamed the modern world. In the meantime, Benedict continued calling those engaged in evangelism 'sects', including Evangelicals in the Global South, not distinguishing between New Religious movements and Evangelical Christianity.

THE TASKS OF POPE FRANCIS

The election of Cardinal Bergoglio to the papacy responds to three basic concerns that the conclave felt it necessary to address. These concerns helped to sketch the profile of the new Pope and Cardinal Bergoglio fitted it. No one in the curia will ever say Benedict XVI's reign was a failure. Yet the impression is that the election of Pope Bergoglio is an implicit admission that the previous papacy achieved less than expected, especially as far as the main point of its agenda was concerned—the relationship with the secular West. After eight years of Benedict's reign, the secular West has become more distant from the Church and critical of it. Moreover, the curial Church has given the poorest performance in its lack of Christian standards. The Church therefore needed a *different* Pope.

Between the traditional yet secularized West and the vibrant yet still 'young' Global South, the conclave has chosen the classical 'via media', or 'middle way'. Pope Bergoglio is an Argentinian born of an Italian family. He is Latin American with a European background. He embodies the transition between the Western establishment and the Southern fervor. Perhaps the conclave thought that choosing an African Pope or an Asian Pope would have been too unsettling. On the other hand, sticking to another European Pope would have been too much of a geo-political conservative move that the Church could not bear. Pope Bergoglio is an in-between figure. Different but not so strange. Similar but not a replica.

He is also a transitional figure. At 76 he is not a 'young' Pope with the expectation of a long papacy. Neither is he an 'old' Pope with not much time in front of him. His papacy will test the willingness of the Church of Rome to move beyond the stand-still position of recent years, but perhaps it will not have enough time to see changes implemented. The conclave did not commit the Roman Catholic Church to a long papacy (like that of John Paul II), but opted to keep the future in sight, waiting to see how this papacy will unfold. All the while, the hierarchy will retain the right to make changes if they deem it necessary.

Pope Bergoglio is presented as an outsider, but he is not. Supported by Cardinal Martini, Bergoglio was the runner up in the 2005 conclave, in which Ratzinger became Benedict XVI. He is well known to the cardinals and was apparently considered 'reliable' by the conclave. In the top list of candidates prior to the conclave was the Brazilian Scherer, another transitional figure. Scherer, however, was apparently perceived as being too much involved in the politics of the Roman curia to be able to free himself from its manoeuvring. Bergoglio is integrated but not organic to the curial world.

The Jesuit Pope chose the name Francis. He mentioned that Francis is a reference to Francis of Assisi (1181–1226). The international press put a lot of stress on this Franciscan symbolism and liked it. Apparently, he will combine Jesuit wit with an emphasis on poverty and frugality. The choice has to do with the willingness to mark an apologetic transition in dealing with the modern world. Ratzinger addressed it by lecturing as a professor, but the West does not like detached, top-down teachers. Ratzinger argued his positions in a clever and intellectual way, but the West is looking more to celebrities who can ignite imagination. Ratzinger denounced the moral relativism of our day, but the West does not like people who do not practice the 'political correctness' of accepting everything. Ratzinger's strategy ended in a stand-still.

Pope Francis began his papacy with a very different apologetic style. Approachable, normal, ordinary, he likes to be with the people, speaking their language and making his message simple. Ratzinger stressed 'faith and reason', Francis is likely to stress 'mercy and simplicity'. Ratzinger addressed the West as theologian, Francis is likely to underline the common humanity of all. The difference is significant.

Will the Church become poor and meek? Will it give priority to a simpler lifestyle? Will it put a stronger emphasis on its spiritual tasks than its secular interests? One thing is to be remembered, Francis of Assisi did not want to reform the whole Church, but wished to receive from the official church the right for his circle of friends to live in poverty. He wanted a niche to pursue his Evangelical ideals, leaving untouched the apparatus of the imperial church. The Church of his time readily gave him what he wanted because she did not feel threatened. We will see whether Pope Francis will transition Evangelical poverty from being a niche of the few idealists to the standard of the worldwide Church. If this is the case, he will have to look at Peter Valdo (1140–1218) who like Francis practiced Evangelical poverty but challenged the official church to do the same. Francis was integrated, Valdo was persecuted.

A final thought on the geo-political significance of the election. Pope Bergoglio comes from a country where, in recent decades, the growth of Evangelical churches and new religious movements of various kinds have shaken the secular *status quo* that saw Roman Catholicism being the dominant religion. This phenomenon designed a new spiritual geography of the country. The same can be said for other Latin American countries. It is interesting that the Roman Catholic Church chose a Pope from Latin America giving him the task of monitoring and presiding over this continental religious border that has become fluid if not weak. The traditional response to the numerical growth of Evangelicals has been labeling them as 'sects' and 'cults', but this derogatory approach did not stop millions of people leaving the Roman Catholic Church. Now, the Pope himself will be directly involved in rescuing the continent. Something important is taking place in Latin America and the risk of losing the continent needed to be addressed at the highest level.

Pope Francis is a transition figure. Time will show how Latin American, curial, Jesuit, and Franciscan he will be. In his first short speech in front of the applauding crowd in St. Peter's square, the most quoted figure was the Virgin Mary to whom he committed himself and his predecessor. His first appointment in his first day of papacy was visiting the Marian basilica of St. Mary Major in Rome to pray to Mary for guidance and help. More of a Jesuit than Franciscan way of beginning a papacy.

THE PAPACY IN SEARCH OF CATHOLICITY

In Roman Catholic understanding, catholicity has to do simultaneously with unity and totality. The basic premise is that multiplicity should be brought into a unity. The Church is seen as an expression, a guarantor and a

In 2007, Latin American Bishops met in Aparecida for their Fifth General Conference, where the then Cardinal Bergoglio was one of the main inspirers of the final document. It is a 165-page text that aptly defines Francis in terms of his theological language, pastoral emphases, and missionary agenda. Aparecida accurately depicts the theological vision of the Pope. For Francis, though, Aparecida is not only a foundational document, it is first and foremost a Marian shrine which was built to keep a statue of Mary that according to tradition was found in 1717 by three fishermen. Since 2011, it has become the greatest Marian pilgrimage destination in the world. During the 2013 World Youth day week, in his speech to the Brazilian Bishops on July 27th, Francis said that 'Aparecida is the interpretative key for the Church's mission.' There is something important to be found there; something that helps in understanding what the Church is all about in terms of its mission. In explaining the intent of his comment, the Pope went on to say that 'in Aparecida God offered Brazil his own mother' and revealed 'his own DNA'.

The Gospel, though, is about God giving His Son to the world, but Francis speaks of God offering his mother. This not merely a matter of theological minutiae! According to the Pope, the lesson of Aparedica has to do with the humility of the fishermen and their zeal to tell others about their discovery. This is the 'interpretative key for the Church's mission': humility and mission. Notice, however, that we are talking about the recovery of a statue of Mary which has become a world-famous attraction for millions of people. The Gospel is about a group of humble fishermen being called by Jesus to follow him and to tell others about Him. Francis is here talking about people who found Mary and became missionaries for her. Again, this is no small difference!

promoter of true unity between God and humanity and within humanity itself. In Vatican II terms, the Church is a 'sacrament of unity'. As long as the institutional structure which preserves this unity remains intact (the Roman element), everything can and must find its home somewhere within its realm (the catholic element).

The Roman Catholic mindset is characterized by an attitude of overall openness without losing touch with its Roman center. It is inherently dynamic and comprehensive, capable of holding together doctrines, ideas and practices that in other Christian traditions are thought of as mutually exclusive. By way of its inclusive et-et (both-and) epistemology, in a catholic system two apparently contradicting elements can be reconciled into a synthesis which entail both. In principle, the system is wide enough to welcome everything and everyone. The defining term is not the Word of God written (*sola Scriptura*) but the Roman Church itself. From a catholic point of view then, affirming something does not necessarily mean denying something else, but simply means enlarging one's perspective of the truth. In this respect, what is perceived as important is the integration of the part into the catholic whole by way of relating the thing newly affirmed with what already exists.

Catholicity allows doctrinal development without a radical breach from the past and also allows different kinds of catholicity to co-exist. Each Pope has his own catholicity project. John Paul II pushed for the church to become a global player, thus expanding geographical catholicity and its profile with the media. Benedict XVI tried to define catholicity in terms of its adherence to universal 'reason', thus trying to remove the chasm between faith and reason that Western Enlightenment had introduced. These catholicity projects are not mutually exclusive, but they all contribute to the overall dynamic catholicity of the Church. They were all organically

related to the Roman element that safeguards the continuity of the system.

After the initial years of his pontificate, it is becoming
apparent what kind of catholicity Francis has in mind. He
wants to build on John Paul II's global catholicity while
shifting emphases from Wojtyła's doctrinal rigidity to
more inclusive patterns. He pays lip service to Ratzinger's
rational catholicity, but wants to move the agenda from
Western ideological battles to 'human' issues which find
appeal across the global spectrum. If Ratzinger wanted
to mark the difference between the Church and the
world, Francis tries to make them overlap. In shaping
the new catholicity he seems closer to the 'pastoral' tone
of John XXIII, who was canonized (i.e. declared a 'saint')
in April 2014. So there is continuity and development.
This is the gist of catholicity.

Francis is seen as a Pope who judges dogma less
important than attitude. Some of his statements (e.g.
'Proselytism is a solemn non-sense', 'Who am I to judge
a homosexual person?', 'Everyone has his own idea of
good and evil and must choose to follow the good and
fight evil as he conceives them') have become slogans that
resonate with secular people. They hardly represent a
Christian view and it is precisely for this reason that
secularists find Francis' 'gospel' a message that is far from
church dogma. It is not an open rejection of it, but it is
understood as a significant move away from it. Francis
has little time for 'non-negotiable' truths, and gives more
attention to the variety of people's conscience. He is more
interested in warmth than light, more in empathy than

judgment. He focuses on attitude rather than identity, and on embracing rather than teaching. He underlines the relational over the doctrinal. For him proximity is more important than integrity. Belonging together has priority over believing differently. Reaching out to people comes before calling them back. Of course, all these marks are not pitted against each other, but their relationship is worked out within a new balance whereby the first one determines the overall orientation. Roman catholicity works this way: never abandoning the past, always enlarging the synthesis by repositioning the elements around the Roman center.

Francis calls this catholicity 'mission'. The word is familiar and intriguing for Bible-believing Christians, yet one needs to understand what he means by it beyond what it appears to mean on the surface.

7

THAT THEY BE ONE

UT UNUM SINT

THE PROSPECTS OF THE PAPACY

Few people know something of the Papacy of the past. More people know the reality of present-day Popes because they see them on television. But what about the Papacy of the future? How will this old institution look in twenty, fifty, or one hundred years? Will it have a future? What shape is the Papacy going to take in the Third Millennium? Is there a place in the global world for this old fashioned, monarchial office in between a religious role and a political function?

There are no easy answers. Several levels are implied in any tentative answer. Are we talking about the better implementation of the Papacy as a government structure without changing its theological claims? Are we referring to finding a new balance between the Papal monarchy and Episcopal collegiality, without subtracting any of the established features of the Papacy? Is a radical reformation of the Papacy possible or even feasible? In the midst of all these questions, one fact must be considered. The institution whose primary task is that of fostering, preserving and expressing Christian unity is a major stumbling block to unity in that at least half of Christians world-wide do not accept it. This is not the only problem surrounding the Papacy. There are still Christians that call the Pope and the Roman Catholic Church to have the courage to implement Biblical reforms that would turn the Papacy upside down.

ROMAN CATHOLIC PROSPECTS

Though encouraging a change of attitude in the modern world, Vatican II did not directly address the doctrine of the Papacy nor its future prospects. It rather confirmed the previous teaching of the Church, Vatican I included. Here is what the Council declares: 'All this teaching about the institution, the perpetuity, the force and reason for the sacred primacy of the Roman Pontiff and of his infallible teaching authority, this sacred Synod again proposes to be firmly believed by all the faithful'.[47] In this sense, Vatican II fully endorsed Vatican I and did not envisage any significant change for the future. According to Roman Catholicism there is something definitive and necessary in the institution of the Papacy, a once-and-for-all nature that is unchangeable because it is a *de iure divino* institution (by divine law). In 1995 John Paul II wrote that 'the Catholic Church is conscious that she has preserved the ministry of the Successor of the Apostle Peter, the Bishop of Rome, whom God established as her perpetual and visible principle and foundation of unity' (*Ut Unun Sint*, 88). Nothing has changed since Trent and Vatican I. The Papacy is a divinely given institution to be accepted as it stands.

The 'spirit' of Vatican II, however, encouraged a new season of openness to talk about controversial issues. As Pope Paul VI recognized in 1967 in his speech to the Secretariat for Christian Unity, 'the Pope, as we well know, is undoubtedly the greatest obstacle in the path of ecumenism'. Never before would a Pope acknowledge that his office was a problem for unity. On the one hand, then, the Pope is the 'perpetual foundation of unity' and, on the other, its 'greatest obstacle'. In ecumenical terms, the present-day issue of the Papacy stands between these two poles: a *de iure* theological necessity and a *de facto* ecumenical impasse.

This awareness of the critical issues around the Papacy was kept alive by subsequent Popes. If Paul VI singled out the question, John Paul II pushed it further and opened up a new scenario. In his already encyclical *Ut Unum Sint* (25th May 1995) John Paul II wrote: 'I am convinced that I have a particular responsibility in this regard, above all in acknowledging the ecumenical aspirations of the majority of the Christian Communities and in heeding the request made of me to find a way of exercising the primacy which, while in no way renouncing what is essential to its mission, is nonetheless open to a new situation' (95). These words stirred an important debate in Roman Catholic and ecumenical circles.[48] Roman Catholic theologians tried to develop ideas and imagine solutions in response to the 'new situation' envisaged by the Pope. Their recurrent questions and concerns have been the following: What does it mean 'exercising the primacy' in a way that does not renounce what is 'essential' while being open to a new 'way' forward? What is 'essential' in the Papacy? What is not? How can the Roman Catholic conviction that the Papacy is an institution given by God be reconciled with the belief that it is also a historical reality which is subject to change and renewal? The debate also saw the Congregation for the Doctrine of the Faith producing a document on 'The Primacy of the Successor of Peter in the Mystery of the Church' in 1998.[49] While reaffirming the traditional understanding of Papacy, this document emphasized its being part of the Episcopal structure of the Church. It therefore suggests that the 'new' way of exercising Papal primacy would be to stress more its Episcopalian character, so a Pope is never isolated from the Bishops and always operates in fellowship with them even when he performs his absolute prerogatives.

So far, Roman Catholic theology, in its official voices and in its wider theological community, has dealt with the issue posed by John Paul II without distancing itself from the traditional view of the Papacy. At most, there has been a timid recognition of past excesses in the way in which Popes of the past exercised their ministry. Moreover, suggestions have been made to expand the powers of the Synod of Bishops and Episcopal Conferences, to limit those of the Roman curia, to implement more 'democratic' procedures in the selection process of new bishops. In other words, the direction of the current debate is an attempt to strike a new balance between the 'center' and the 'periphery' of the Church, and to put more checks and balances in the system without altering it in any significant way.

Francis is viewed as a Pope who will 'reform' the Papacy. Since his election, Francis has been sending messages that he wants to stress the role of the Bishop of Rome rather than the more universal and political ones, but leaving the overall system intact. It is a matter of emphasis, not of theological substance. The only 'new' developments which are envisaged so far remain within the existing theological framework of the Papacy and do not bring any real change. Perhaps this is what John Paul II had in mind and what the Roman Catholic Church can afford theologically.

'Has Christ been divided?' This is the question that Paul rhetorically asks the Corinthians (1 Cor. 1:13). It is also the question that Pope Francis commented upon in his homily at the end of the 2014 Week of Prayer for Christian Unity at the Basilica of St. Paul Outside the Walls in Rome. The first remark has to do with the understanding of unity as a 'goal'. In commenting on the developments of the ecumenical movement, he spoke of 'journeying together on the road towards unity,' implying the idea that unity stands ahead of us as if it were a goal to be eventually reached. Unity is therefore in the future tense. What exactly does unity mean here and why is it in the future? Later, the Pope made a comment that sheds light on these issues. He referred to the prospect of 'restoration of full visible unity among all Christians' as the future climax of the ecumenical path. It is necessary, however, to unpack such a statement. Firstly there is the idea of 'restoration.' According to this view, there was a time in the life of the church when full and visible unity existed. It is not explicitly stated here, but what is perhaps referred to is the 'undivided' First Millennium of the church before the East-West Schism (1054 AD) and the Protestant Reformation of the sixteenth century. This view is common in ecumenical circles, but highly problematic from historical and theological points of view. From its early years, the church has constantly been dealing with divisions and conflicts, as the Pauline text testifies. Before there was a Pope and even after the papacy came into existence, a 'golden age' of Christian unity never existed, not even within the Roman Catholic Church! Unity always stands in tension and under attack. Rather than restoring unity, the Bible urges us to 'maintain' the already given unity (Ephesians 4:3) and to equip the body of Christ in order to 'attain' the unity of faith (4:13). In other words, from the beginning of the church, unity is a given and a goal. It is a gift and a task. The restoration model wrongly implies that unity was full in the first stages of the church and was then lost along the way, and now needs to be recovered. Christian unity is instead a given reality amongst those whom the Father has given to the Son (John 17:9) that must be protected from sinful disruption and lived out in visible ways according to biblical principles.[50] Secondly, the Pope made reference to a 'full' and 'visible' unity as the goal of ecumenism. According to the Roman Catholic view, 'full' means sacramentally full, i.e. same baptism, same eucharist, same ministry. Given the self-understanding of the Roman Church, it means adhering and submitting to the sacramental theology of Rome and the hierarchical nature of its priesthood. 'Visible' means that unity needs to accept the visible Papal structure of the Roman Catholic Church as the divinely appointed way for the One Church of Christ. The ecumenical price for full and visible unity is the acceptance of the Roman Catholic view of the Church. All other views are defective and, in the end, partial and invisible.

ECUMENICAL AND INTER-FAITH PROJECTS

As already pointed out, the Papacy was and still is one of the stumbling blocks of the ecumenical movement. The willingness of John Paul II to find new ways of exercising the primacy, however, has attracted lots of attention from other Churches (i.e. Eastern Orthodox Churches) and Ecclesial Communities (e.g. Protestant Churches and movements).[51] The debate around the Papacy has become one of the most discussed topics in ecumenical theology and various proposals have been explored.[52]

Each Christian tradition brings to the discussion its own theological and historical perspective. Orthodox churches do not accept the 'primacy of jurisdiction' (i.e. binding power that demands obedience) that implies the superiority of the Bishop of Rome over other bishops and, in their understanding, undermines the collegiality of Churches. These Churches already recognize the Pope as the Bishop of Rome and the Patriarch of the Western Church. They are open to acknowledging him a 'primacy of honor' (*primus inter pares*, first among equals), always functioning within the fellowship of other Bishops and as the spokesperson of the whole Church when decisions are the result of consensus. Some voices in this debate argue that the Papacy should look for inspiration at the ways in which the Papal primacy was implemented in the First Millennium of the Church, prior to the Eastern Schism (1054). As it worked out then, so it should work out today, the argument goes. The primary problem with this is that it is too idealist to be feasible. Most problems associated with the Papacy arouse in the Second Millennium, and the last dogmatic pronouncement of the Roman Catholic Church on the Papacy (Vatican I, 1870) simply objectified them. Can Rome turn the clock back to the First Millennium, thus admitting to have made a mistake with Papal infallibility?

Ecumenical Protestant Churches find it impossible to accept the theological framework of the Papacy and the traditional forms in which the Papal office has been exercised throughout the centuries. Leaving aside theological arguments and historical forms, they are inclined to believe that in the globalized world a global Christian spokesperson would be practically useful for Christianity as a whole. In the present-day ecumenical scene the Roman Pope is best suited to perform such a service, even outside Roman Catholic circles. According to this view, no 'primacy of jurisdiction' should be recognized outside of the Roman Catholic Church. The only authority of the Pope over non-Catholics would be a kind of *auctoritas*, a spontaneous, bottom-up, and flexible influence, not *potestas*, a top-down, imposed and binding power. The future Pope could act like a leader who is commissioned to represent the Christian Churches before the public, according to a specific mandate assigned to him. Protestant ecumenism is looking to find a way to make it possible for non-Catholic Churches to be *cum Petro* (with Peter) without being *sub Petro* (under Peter). Whether or not this distinction is acceptable for Roman Catholicism remains to be seen. It is hard to imagine a 'light' Papacy in which the Pope self-limits himself, declaring Vatican I obsolete and becoming the informal spokesperson of a world-wide cluster of churches without claiming any authority over them.

The debate on the prospects of the Papacy is not confined to ecumenical circles. Since present-day Popes are global figures, well known far beyond the borders of Christianity, the discussion has taken an inter-faith dimension too. A boost towards it was the 1986 Day of

Prayer for Peace convened in Assisi by John Paul II when 160 religious leaders from around the world and from a wide spectrum of religious traditions took part. In these inter-faith circles, the Pope is increasingly considered to be the highest representative of Christianity and the most authoritative figure in the religious world. Some religious leaders (e.g. from the Muslim world) go as far as saying that the Pope represents the whole of humanity when he advocates for the poor of the world or when he makes appeals for peace. The symbolic importance of the Pope as embodying the unity of mankind further stretches the Papacy into a pan-religious service. The fact that many secular people, though not recognizing the outward religious elements of the Papacy, are ready to acclaim the

(?) Who does the Pope represent? In the interview book *Light of the World: The Pope, the Church, and the Signs of the Times* (San Francisco, CA: Ignatius Press, 2010) Peter Seewald wanted to know what Pope Benedict XVI thought of his Petrine ministry that causes trouble for non-Catholic Christians. Well, agreement about the papal ministry with Orthodox churches is not so far away, said Ratzinger. Yet there is another facet to it. More and more, he said, religious leaders are realizing that in the global world a global voice is needed to address the importance of 'religious values' and the disruptive claims of secularism. Being the 'single voice on great themes' is what the Pope emeritus envisaged for the papal ministry: for Catholics and non-Catholics alike, as well as for Muslims, Hindus, etc. The Pope offered his ministry to serve as the spokesperson for all religious-minded peoples of the world. This is the vast frontier development of the papacy that embraces both ecumenism and inter-religious dialogue. Of course this is not the full scope of the RC understanding of the papal office, but it will pave the way to achieving it.

Pope as a 'star' (at least when he makes politically correct statements) is a further indication that the contours of the debate over the future of the Papacy go far beyond the traditional intra-ecclesiastical boundaries. The world, religious and secular, seems to need a global figure that no political institution and no international organization can provide at the moment. Could the Papacy become such a universal leadership structure?

EVANGELICAL SKEPTICISM

After Vatican II (1962–5) and the Lausanne Congress on World Evangelization (1974) a new phase of dialogue was inaugurated between Evangelicals and the Roman Catholic Church.[53] From the historical opposition between the two constituencies, their relationship began to be marked by frank conversation and friendly debate. The doctrine of the Papacy was recognized as part of the unsolved theological issues, in the area of the status of the teaching authority of the Church,[54] or in the different understandings of the apostolic succession.[55] It is true that in more recent years there has been an Evangelical fascination with the last three Popes. In this sense Evangelicals seem to reflect the wider celebrity culture that wants to focus on a 'star'.

From a more comprehensive theological point of view, the 1986 document entitled *Evangelical Perspective on Roman Catholicism* by the World Evangelical Fellowship represents the first (and perhaps the only) authoritative Evangelical statement after Vatican II that has a detailed section on the Papacy.[55] The document reflects standard yet persisting conservative Protestant concerns over foundational aspects of Roman Catholic doctrine such as mariology, authority in the church, the Papacy and infallibility, justification by faith, sacramentalism and the Eucharist. As far as the Papacy is concerned, after surveying the main issues at stake, the document is worth quoting at length: 'Scripture leaves no room for mere corrections on the Roman Catholic doctrine of the papacy. It compels us to reject the idea of Petrine primacy as the basis for papal infallibility. The New Testament is not concerned to elevate Peter above the other apostles, nor to institute an enduring 'office of Peter'; nor did Peter himself ever suggest it (1 Peter 5:1–4). Truth and unity are far better served by the confession of the unique lordship of Jesus Christ than in any other way. Under the kingship of Jesus Christ as the sole and supreme Head of the Church, we as Evangelicals seek to honour the subservient role of God's people in the governance of the church, through the exercise of the priesthood of all believers, within the biblical patterns of church governement. The papacy, with its claim to infallibility, stands in the way of renewal within Roman Catholicism. It also poses an immense obstacle to Christian unity. It prevents, moreover, an obedient listening to the voice of the one true Lord of the church. The doctrine of papal infallibility is therefore not a 'divinely revealed dogma' which 'all Christians must believe'. It is rather an idea which no Christian can accept without denying the teachings of the infallible Scriptures.[57]

While the Evangelical document welcomes the new phase that Roman Catholicism is experiencing after Vatican II and hopes for further steps particularly brought about by the Biblical movement, it also reiterates a traditional, clear-cut Evangelical critique. The dividing line between Evangelicals and Roman Catholics will be unresolved until 'a reformation according to the Word of God' takes place in the Church of Rome.[58]

We are back to square one. The whole process that led to the formation of the Papacy started from faulty Biblical foundations. It then grew following imperial patterns and political interests. Instead of self-questioning in the light of the Word of God, it was given a dogmatic outlook and infallible status at Vatican I. Now it tries to find new forms for itself without changing anything essential that was accumulated. It continues to grow out of its spurious start. The only revision that is necessary is to go back to the Scriptures and be willing to follow its teaching, no matter what the cost.

BIBLIOGRAPHY

REFERENCE WORKS

F.J. Coppa (ed.), *Encyclopedia of the Vatican and Papacy* (Westport, CT: Greenwood Press, 1999).

J.N.D. Kelly, *Oxford Dictionary of Popes*, 2th edition (Oxford: Oxford University Press, 2006).

R.P. McBrien, *Lives of the Popes. The Pontiffs from St. Peter to John Paul II* (New York, NY: HarperOne, 1997).

HISTORICAL WORKS

G. Denzler, *Das Papsttum: Geschichte und Gegenwart* (München: C.H. Beck'sche Verlagbuchhandlung, 1997).

E. Duffy, *Saints and Sinners. A History of the Popes* (New Haven, CT: Yale University Press, 1997).

J. Grau, *Catolicismo Romano. Origines y Desarrollo*, 2th edition (Barcelona: Ediciones Evangelicas Europeas, 1987).

J.J. Norwich, *Absolute Monarchs. A History of the Papacy* (New York, NY: Random House Trade Paperbacks, 2011).

J. O'Malley, *A History of the Popes. From Peter to the Present* (Lanham, MD: Sheed & Ward, 2010).

C. Papini, *Da vescovo di Roma a sovrano del mondo* (Torino: Claudiana, 2009); Id., *Origine e sviluppo del potere temporale dei papi (650–850)*, (Torino: Claudiana, 2013).

A.D. Wright, *The Early Modern Papacy. From the Council of Trent to the French Revolution, 1564–1789* (Harlow: Longman, 1999).

THEOLOGICAL WORKS

Il primato del successore di Pietro. Atti del simposio teologico (Città del Vaticano: Libreria Editrice Vaticana, 1998).

Gregg R. Allison, *Roman Catholic Theology and Practice. An Evangelical Assessment* (Wheaton, IL: Crossway, 2014) ch. 5

N.L. Geisler & J.M. Betancourt, *Is Rome the True Church? A Consideration of the Roman Catholic Claim* (Wheaton, IL: Crossway, 2008).

R.R. Reymond, *The Reformation's Conflict with Rome. Why It Must Continue* (Fearn: Mentor, 2001) pp. 29–66.

K. Schatz, *Papal Primacy From Its Origins to the Present* (Collegeville, MN: Liturgical Press 1996).

R.C. Sproul, *Are We Together? A Protestant Analyzes Roman Catholicism* (Sandford, FL: Reformation Trust Publishing, 2012) pp. 85–100.

ENDNOTES

1. *Evangelical Theological Perspectives on Post-Vatican II Roman Catholicism* (Bern-Oxford: Peter Lang, 2003).

2. www.vaticanfiles.org

3. Quotations will be taken by *Catechism of the Catholic Church* (London: Geoffrey Chapman, 1994). The electronic text can be found at www.vatican.va/archive/ENG0015/_INDEX.HTM.

4. The first paragraph of John Paul II , Apostolic Constitution *Universi Dominici Gregis* (22 February 1996).

5. Dogmatic Constitution on the Church, *Lumen Gentium*, 18. There are various published editions of the Vatican II documents. The texts can be accessed at www.vatican.va/archive/hist_councils/ii_vatican_council/documents/vat-ii_const_19641121_lumen-gentium_en.html.

6. According to the *Catechism of the Catholic Church*, sacraments are 'efficacious signs of grace, instituted by Christ and entrusted to the Church, by which divine life is dispensed to us. The visible rites by which the sacraments are celebrated signify and make present the graces proper to each sacrament' (1131).

7. A. Paravicini Bagliani, *Le Chiavi e la Tiara. Immagini e simboli del papato medievale* (Roma: Viella, 1998).

8. A Biblical account of the Biblical foundations of the Papacy is given by Vatican II's Dogmatic Constitution of the Church, *Lumen Gentium*, 19–24.

9. On the person and significance of Peter in the NT, cf. the pastoral portrait by E. Donnelly, *Peter: Eyewitness of His Majesty as Disciple, Preacher, Pastor* (Edinburgh: The Banner of Truth Trust, 1998) and the more scholarly volume by L.R. Helyer, *The Life and Witness of Peter* (Downers Grove, IL: IVP – Nottingham: Apollos 2012).

10. The standard survey of the interpretation of the passage is the volume by O. Cullmann, *Peter: Disciple, Apostle, Martyr. A Historical and Theological Study* (Philadelphia: Westminster Press, 1962). More recent discussions are analyzed by M. Bockmuehl, *Simon Peter in Scripture and Memory. The New Testament Apostle in the Early Church* (Grand Rapids, MI: Baker Academic, 2012).

11. This reading was argued for by V. Subilia, *Tu sei Pietro. L'enigma del fondamento evangelico del papato* (Turin: Claudiana, 1978) and more recently by M. Hengel, *Saint Peter: The Underestimated Apostle* (Grand Rapids, MI: Eerdmans, 2010).

12. For extended exegetical discussions on the passage, cf. W. Hendriksen, *Matthew* (Edinburgh: The Banner of Truth Trust, 1974, reprint 1989) pp. 641–652; R.T. France, *The Gospel of Matthew* NICNT (Grand Rapids, MI: Eerdmans, 2002) pp. 611–628.

13. For more exegetical discussions, see L. Morris, *The Gospel According to John* NICNT, revised edition (Grand Rapids, MI: Eerdmans, 1995) pp. 757–775 and D.A. Carson, *The Gospel According to John* PNTC (Grand Rapids, MI: Eerdmans, 1991) pp. 675–686.

14. H.J. Pottmeyer, *The Petrine Ministry in a Changing Church*, 'Tablet' (September 14th, 1996) pp. 188–190.

15. *Ad Romanos* I,1.

16. e.g. *Against Heresies*, 3:3:2. Other patristic sources are collected by R.B. Eno, *The Rise of the Papacy* (Wilmington, DE: Glazier, 1990) and J.-M.R. Tillard, *The Bishop of Rome* (London: SPCK, 1983).

17. See M. Grant, *The Emperor Constantine* (London: Weidenfeld & Nicolson, 1993).

18. This whole transitional time is masterly dealt with by P. Brown, *The Rise of Western Christendom. Triumph and Diversity, AD 200–1000* (Cambridge, MA: Harvard University Press, 1966).

19. P. Prodi, *The Papal Prince. One Body and Two Souls: The Papal Monarchy in Early Modern Europe* (Cambridge: Cambridge University Press, 1988). See also T.F.X. Noble, *The Republic of St. Peter. The Birth of the Papal State* (Philadelphia, PA: University of Pennsylvania Press, 1984).

20. J. Ratzinger, *Principles of Catholic Theology* (San Francisco, CA: Ignatius, 1987) p. 196.

21. F. Oakley, *The Conciliarist Tradition* (Oxford: Oxford University Press, 2003).

22. On this whole period, see C.M.D. Crowder, *Unity, Heresy, and Reform, 1378–1460: The Conciliar Response to the Great Schism* (New York, NY: St. Martin's Press, 1977) and A. Landi, *Concilio e papato nel Rinascimento, 1449–1516* (Torino: Claudiana, 1997).

23. J. Riley-Smith, *The Crusades. A History*, 2nd edition (London: Continuum, 2005).

24. J.F. D'Amico, *Renaissance Humanism in Papal Rome: Humanists and Churchmen on the Eve of the Reformation*, 2nd edition (Baltimore, MD: Johns Hopkins University, 1991).

25. *De Romano Pontifice* (1586) I,3.

26. 'Differing Attitudes Towards Papal Primacy' (1973). The text can be accessed at www.usccb.org/beliefs-and-teachings/ecumenical-and-interreligious/ecumenical/lutheran/attitudes-papal-primacy.cfm and is a useful summary of the main controversial issues around the Papacy between present-day Lutherans and Roman Catholics.

27. P. Ricca, *Lutero e il Papa* in G. Alberigo et all., *Lutero nel suo e nel nostro tempo* (Torino: Claudiana, 1983) pp. 169–200. Further elements can be found in R. Bäumer, *Martin Luther und der Papst* (Münster: Aschendorff, 1970).

28. On Calvin's views of Rome as they are presented in various writings, see M. Stolk, *Calvin and Rome* in H.J. Selderhuis (ed.), *The Calvin Handbook* (Grand Rapids, MI: Eerdmans, 2009) pp. 104–112.

29. This word 'antidote' would come back in Calvin's refutations of

the Acts of the Council of Trent. See his *Acta synodi Tridentinae cum Antidoto* (1547).

30. See also Calvin's *Institutes* IV,6–7.

31. See my paper 'Separazione e riforma della Chiesa ne 'Il Trattato della vera Chiesa e della necessità di viver in essa", A. Oliveri and P. Bolognesi (eds.), *Pietro Martire Vermigli (1499–1562). Umanista, Riformatore, Pastore* (Rome: Herder, 2003) pp. 225–232.

32. It is followed by *The Savoy Declaration* (1658), art. XXVI and *The London Baptist Confession of Faith* (1689), art. XXVI. See J.R. Beeke & S.B. Ferguson (eds.), *Reformed Confessions Harmonized* (Grand Rapids, MI: Baker Publ. Book, 1999).

33. The 7th *Disputation* was published as F. Turretin, *Whether It Can be Proven the Pope of Rome is the Antichrist*, ed. by R. Winburn (Forestville, CA: Protestant Reformation Publications, 1999).

34. See M. Roberts, *Francis Turretine on the Antichrist*, 'The Banner of Truth' 335–336 (Aug–Sept 1991) pp. 1–8.

35. G. Fragnito, *La Bibbia al rogo. La censura ecclesiastica e i volgarizzamenti della Scrittura, 1471–1605* (Bologna: il Mulino, 1997). More recently the same scholar edited the volume *Church, Censorship and Culture in Early Modern Italy* (Cambridge: Cambridge University Press, 2001).

36. The Congregation's name was changed to 'Sacred Congregation for the Doctrine of the Faith' at the end of the Second Vatican Council (1965). In 1985 the adjective 'sacred' was dropped and is now known as the 'Congregation for the Doctrine of the Faith'. Its task is 'to promote and safeguard the doctrine on faith and morals in the whole Catholic world' according to John Paul II, Apostolic Constitution *Pastor Bonus*, 48 (28 June 1988).

37. M.D.W. Jones, *The Counter-Reformation: Religion and Society in Early Modern Europe* (Cambridge: Cambridge University Press, 1995). Other scholarship prefers to speak of 'Catholic renewal' to indicate the rather independent nature of the Catholic renewal movement from the Protestant Reformation, i.e. R.P. Hsia, *The World of Catholic Renewal 1540–1770* (Cambridge: Cambridge University Press, 1998). Was the Catholic Reformation a reaction against Protestantism or was it an

inner dynamic that was chiefly driven by internal forces? Beyond the use of words, the dispute has far-reaching implications.

38. O. Chadwick, *The Popes and European Revolution* (Oxford: Oxford University Press, 1981).

39. A.B. Hasler, *How the Pope Became Infallible. Pius IX and the Politics of Persuasion* (New York, NY: Doubleday, 1981). A critical reading of the dogma of Papal infallibility is also offered by H. Küng, *Infallible? An Inquiry* (New York, NY: Doubleday, 1983).

40. The reference work for the Social Doctrine of the church is the *Compendium of the Social Doctrine of the Church* (2004): http://www.vatican.va/roman_curia/pontifical_councils/justpeace/documents/rc_pc_justpeace_doc_20060526_compendio-dott-soc_en.html. See my paper *La doctrine sociale de l'Église catholique romaine*, 'Théologie Évangélique' 6/1 (2007) pp. 51–66.

41. A comparison between Leo XIII and Kuyper can be found in J. Bolt, 'The Social Question and the Social Gospel: Abraham Kuyper, Walter Rauschenbush, and Leo XIII' in Id., *A Free Church, A Holy Nation* (Grand Rapids, MI: W.B. Eerdmans, 2001) pp. 227–255.

42. G. Weigel, *Evangelical Catholicism. Deep Reform in the 21st-century Church* (New York, NY: Basic Books, 2013). This book is an attempt of re-defining what Evangelical means away from its Biblical, historical, and theological meaning and towards a sociological and psychological understanding that fits the dogmas and practices of Roman Catholicism.

43. Tim Perry (ed.), *The Legacy of John Paul II: An Evangelical Assessment* (Downers Grove, IL: IVP, 2007).

44. Timothy George, pp. 309–312.

45. Jim Packer, p. 8.

46. Further elements can be found in my paper, *Progressive, Conservative or Roman Catholic? On the Theology of Joseph Ratzinger in Evangelical Perspective*, 'Perichoresis' 6.2 (2008) pp. 201–218.

47. Dogmatic Constitution of the Church, *Lumen Gentium*, 18.

48. E.g. P. Hünermann (ed.), *Papstamt und Ökumene: Zum Petrusdienst an der Einheit aller Getauften* (Regensburg: F. Pustet, 1997); H.J. Pottmeyer, *Towards a Papacy in Communion: Perspectives from Vatican Councils I and II* (New York, NY: Crossroad Publ. Co, 1998); J.R. Quinn,

The Reform of the Papacy. The Costly Call to Christian Unity (New York, NY: Herder & Herder, 1999).

49. www.vatican.va/roman_curia/congregations/cfaith/documents/rc_con_cfaith_doc_19981031_primato-successore-pietro_en.html

50. See John M. Frame, *Evangelical Reunion. Denominations and the Body of Christ* (Grand Rapids, MI: Baker 1991).

51. Roman Catholic ecclesiology distinguishes between Churches that have true sacraments and, because of the apostolic succession, the priesthood and the Eucharist, and Ecclesial Communities who have broken the apostolic succession.

52. A survey of the ecumenical dialogue on the Papacy is offered by A. Garuti, *The Primacy of the Bishop of Rome and the Ecumenical Dialogue* (San Francisco, CA: Ignatius Press, 2004) and G. Cereti, *Le chiese cristiane di fronte al papato. Il ministero petrino del vescovo di Roma nei documenti del dialogo ecumenico* (Bologna: EDB, 2006).

53. For an introductory survey, see my paper *Evangelicals and the Roman Catholic Church since Vatican II*, 'European Journal of Theology' X (2001/1) pp. 25–35.

54. John Stott – Basil Meeking (eds.), *The Evangelical – Roman Catholic Dialogue on Mission 1977–1984* (Grand Rapids, MI – Exeter: Eerdmans – Paternoster, 1986) Ch. 1.

55. Charles Colson – Richard J. Neuhaus (eds.), *Evangelicals and Catholics Together. Toward a Common Mission* (Dallas, TX: Word Publ., 1995).

56. Published in *Evangelical Review of Theology* 10:4 (1986) 343–364 and 11:1 (1987) 78–94 as well as by P. Schrotenboer (ed.), *Roman Catholicism. A Contemporary Evangelical Perspective* (Grand Rapids: Baker Books, 1987). The World Evangelical Fellowship is now the World Evangelical Alliance (WEA).

57. 'Evangelical Review of Theology' (1986) p. 364.

58. 'Evangelical Review of Theology' (1987) p. 93.

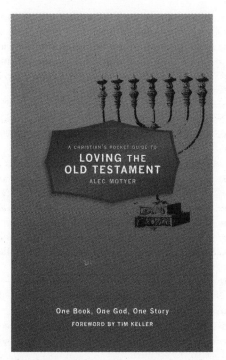

A CHRISTIAN'S POCKET GUIDE TO

LOVING THE OLD TESTAMENT

ALEC MOTYER

One Book, One God, One Story

FOREWORD BY TIM KELLER

Many of us know and love the stories and characters of the Old Testament such as Joseph, Moses and Jonah. But how do we view its importance in relation to New Testament teaching and our 21st century experiences? This accessible yet powerful addition to the Pocket Guide series draw together the threads of Scripture to help us understand the power of God's word when viewed in its completeness.

ISBN: 978-1-78191-580-6

Christian Focus Publications

Our mission statement –

STAYING FAITHFUL
In dependence upon God we seek to impact the world through literature faithful to His infallible Word, the Bible. Our aim is to ensure that the Lord Jesus Christ is presented as the only hope to obtain forgiveness of sin, live a useful life and look forward to heaven with Him.

Our books are published in four imprints:

CHRISTIAN FOCUS

Popular works including biographies, commentaries, basic doctrine and Christian living.

CHRISTIAN HERITAGE

Books representing some of the best material from the rich heritage of the church.

MENTOR

Books written at a level suitable for Bible College and seminary students, pastors, and other serious readers. The imprint includes commentaries, doctrinal studies, examination of current issues and church history.

CF4·K

Children's books for quality Bible teaching and for all age groups: Sunday school curriculum, puzzle and activity books; personal and family devotional titles, biographies and inspirational stories – Because you are never too young to know Jesus!

Christian Focus Publications Ltd,
Geanies House, Fearn, Ross-shire,
IV20 1TW, Scotland, United Kingdom.
www.christianfocus.com